GREAT SPECKLED BIRD

Great Speckled Bird

CONFESSIONS OF A VILLAGE PREACHER

Rob McCall

Rob McCall (signature)

PUSHCART

ISBN: 978-1-888889-67-3

Pushcart Press
P.O. Box 380
Wainscott, New York 11975

Distributed by W.W. Norton Co.
500 Fifth Avenue
New York, New York 10110

Designed by Mary Kornblum, CMYK DESIGN INC.

PRINTED IN THE UNITED STATES OF AMERICA

To Rebecca

CONTENTS

Prelude

Spring

Summer

Fall

Winter

Postlude

Prelude

Prelude

A Letter to the Reader

Dear Reader,

This volume is a confession of heresy, of failure, of arrogance, of blindness, of stubborn-ness—mine and others'. It is also a confession of faith: in people, in Nature, in the Creator, and in a very old and very good way of life—village life.

First confession: I am not a Christian by any prevailing definition. Christians can say the Apostle's Creed without crossing their fingers. They believe in the second coming of Christ and the resurrection of the body. Christians are sure that accepting Jesus Christ as their personal Lord and Savior will gain them a place in heaven. Christians believe that God is three in one, Father, Son and Holy Ghost. Christians believe that Christ was born of a virgin, with no earthly father. Christians are confident that theirs is the only way, and do not hesitate to convert others by force or guile. Christians believe that humanity and the Earth are fallen and can only be redeemed by Christ. They believe that animals have no souls and that mankind is master of the Earth.

3

*All my life I have read the same scriptures, prayed the
same prayers and sung the same hymns as other Christians,
but I have been led another way. I do not believe these
things. Nor do I find much evidence that Jesus believed these
things, either.*

*There is an Old Faith that survives out in the country,
in small towns, tribal reserves, and the hearts of spiritual
people all over the globe who want little to do with organized religion. It is the faith that was from the beginning. It
is faith in the earth and the weather, the sun and moon, the
land and the sea. It's anchored in the fertility of the earth and
the changing of the seasons. It acknowledges the first Mother
and first Father, male and female. It celebrates the healing
power of the Creator spirit. It holds to the faith of the ancestors and works to pass that faith on to coming generations.
It has two natural laws: "You reap what you sow," and "Do
to others as you would have others do to you." It has many
teachers. It is the original faith of humankind and will never
be extinguished.*

*Organized religions, born in the cities, have stolen from
the Old Faith and then tried to stamp it out. But the Old
Faith lives on, quietly and joyfully, in the country. That is
why it is called 'pagan' and 'heathen.' Pagan comes from the
Latin word for country; heathen means from the wilderness.*

*The Old Faith has no need for bishops or popes, celibates,
catechisms, dogma, or inquisitions. Its cathedrals are the
mountains and the shores. Its temple is roofed by clouds and
illuminated by the lights in the sky. Everyone is a priest.*

*When I was younger I felt sorry for Native Americans
whose old faith was over-ruled and dominated by organized
religion four or five hundred years ago. I still do. But, after
many years, the realization came that my people's old faith
was over-ruled in the British Isles fifteen hundred years
ago or more. White people have been separated from their*

old faith much longer, and have almost given in; but not completely.

If, when you hear Native American or Celtic or African or other tribal music, you get excited, it is because of the Old Faith still alive in you, the original soul and spirit, which will never die, and will always come to life again as sure as spring follows winter. We hear it in the fiddles and pipes, and the rattles and the drums. This is the Old Faith that always springs forth hopeful.

The Old Faith does not give men dominion over women. Women are not limited to being either virgins or witches. Women are the source of new life and the teachers of the young. Women are equal to men in the Old Faith, which honors both the circle and the cross, the earth and the four directions. It does not sacrifice children or animals to an angry deity. Its fundamental creed is life, not death. Its doctrine is love, not fear. It is satisfied with making the earth better for present and coming generations, not obsessed with what happens after we die, since we cannot know this. It wants a better present for all creatures, not just a better future in heaven for a select few who know the magic words and the secret rituals.

The Old Faith is quietly but vigorously alive in the country, small towns, tribal villages, and reservations all over the world. You can see its seasonal symbols everywhere if you have the eyes for it. See the orange and black of the harvest. See the green and red wreathes and evergreen trees at the beginning of winter. See the handmade baskets and herbal remedies. See the flowers of spring, the lilies and daffodils. See the gardens and orchards and wildflowers in bloom.

The Old Faith is not written only in books to be read by the elect and elite. It is declared far and wide to every creature in the Creation we behold. See the sun through the year as it goes higher in the sky, then lower, until it rises again.

Hear the birds sing to the dawn. Theirs is the same old faith as ours. Watch the flowers turn their faces to the sun as it moves across the sky. Theirs too is the Old Faith. See the moon through its monthly changes and watch the tides rising and falling with it. This is the one original ancient faith, eons older than what Christians call the "old-time religion."

The organized religions of books, cities, and churches are breaking down all around. They are utterly bankrupt. Look at the disintegration of the "Catholic" church with its accumulated wealth and perversion, impoverishing and debasing the faithful while enriching and indulging the hierarchy. Look at the mainline Protestant churches with their fleeing multitudes and lukewarm faith. Look at the fundamentalists of all religions obsessed with fear and violence, desperately seeking the suicidal end of this world they so bitterly hate. All these organized religions are coming to an end.

Yet, we in whom the Old Faith still lives are afraid of practicing it, though plants and other animals practice it fearlessly day and night, summer and winter. Why are we afraid? The Old Faith has been brutally suppressed for thousands of years. Crusades, conquistadors, religious wars, inquisitions and burning at the stake, angry men with their punishing colonization of the earth and the human spirit have done everything they could to suppress the Ancient Faith. We have an ancestral fear of practicing it in the open, so we practice covertly behind closed doors or far out in the country where it still rules.

Today, the earth is being ravaged, the oceans are dying, the ice-caps are melting, whole species are becoming extinct, diseases like HIV/AIDS and malaria are visiting destruction among humans greater than anything since the Black Death, from the selfish pride of un-natural, urban, hierarchical religions erasing the ancient wisdom of the Creator and the Old Faith, and imposing rigors of the book to enrich and empower the few at the expense of the many. This is the work of demonic powers and principalities, kingdoms of this world trying to seize the power of the Creator for their own purposes.

It is time for the Old Faith to come out in the open and return to the prophets who preached about the vineyard taken away from those who would enrich themselves and given to those who would use it to enrich others. Jesus never meant to start a new religion of gilded cathedrals, popes and bishops. He called down the laws and creeds of temple religion to return to the Old Faith. "Love God with all your heart, soul, mind and strength," he said, "and love your neighbor as yourself." He called down the Roman Empire for its slavery and exploitation, and was tortured to death by it in the most hideous way. But, like the Old Faith, he did not die.

To you whose religion is fishing or farming or gardening or handicraft or hiking or fiddling or drumming; to you whose saints are your neighbors and children, to you whose temple is the earth and whose creed is the turning of the seasons; to you whose matins are sung by the birds and whose evensong is the rising moon and the setting sun; to you who remember and remain fearless and joyful in the Old Faith: Have courage. Your hour approaches. You are to be the redemption of the world.

Rob McCall
Blue Hill, Maine

THE GREAT SPECKLED BIRD

———◆———

The mad prophet Jeremiah gave us the great speckled bird soaring over the wilderness, harassed but untroubled, like an eagle mobbed by crows but still holding its unwavering course. Many times I have walked down toward the lonely gravel shore by our camp on Cobscook Bay, and just as I was about to pass under the biggest black spruce, a bald eagle would drop out of its high branches, like a plains Eagle Dancer in full regalia, and fall toward the water with spread wings bigger than a man. Primal fear, joy and wonder together would fill my chest as the winged shadow sailed above me, to beat its enormous wings over the water, then to rise and disappear into a tiny speck in the sky. I had witnessed the angel of life and death.

Bald Eagles are gaining on the Maine coast. They may have a wingspread of eight feet. Their nests – usually built in the broken top of a tall pine or spruce on the water—may be eight feet wide, twelve feet high and weigh more than a ton. Their prey includes fish, ducks, young deer or other mammals, and carrion. The adult is brown with white head and tail. The adolescent may be as large as the adult but is speckled. Both are majestic and horrible.

Often I will look up from my work to the high-pitched whistling call of an eagle pair and see them soaring a mile up in a circle around the sun. At times like these, I am open to a message from on high, and I'm rarely disappointed. The soul is softened to receive it by the majestic sacred geometry of earth, man, sky, eagle, sun.

The Bald Eagle, the Great Speckled Bird of the Bible, the Roc of the Arabian Nights, the Griffin, the Thunderbird, the B-movie pterodactyl; all call up the same awe at the great cloud-born creature who could shelter us under soft wings, or seize us in cruel talons, rise on mighty wings, and drop us to be dashed on the rocks so our bones could be picked clean. It is the flying shadow of bombers over Dresden and Hiroshima, or airliners over the World Trade Center, or Predator drones over the Afghan desert. It is also the soft, silent wings of grievous angels come to carry us gently away to paradise.

Rev. Guy Smith wrote the gospel song, "The Great Speckled Bird," popularized by Roy Acuff, in 1936 suggesting an interpretation of Jeremiah 12:9: that the Biblical bird was the church, harassed and persecuted by unbelievers. Maybe that's what Jeremiah meant; maybe it wasn't. I think it wasn't. Maybe Rev. Smith's parishioners or family were outraged about something, and he thought it was all about him and started feeling persecuted, which preachers are sometimes inclined to do.

The mystery of Jeremiah's imagery is that we don't really know what that Great Speckled Bird is. Jeremiah himself didn't know. Prophets, like poets, leave the interpretation of their ecstatic utterances to others. Look it up if you have a Bible. The Speckled Bird could be the prophet. It could be the Lord. It could be the nation of Israel. It could be a bald eagle, an osprey, a great blue heron, a turkey vulture, a condor or a black-backed gull. Or it could be an angel.

Back before there were so many raging fundamentalists, back before the niggling literalists began insisting that every word of the Bible must be read as science, nearly everyone read the scriptures as artful poetry. Like the cave paintings at Lascaux or the monoliths of Stonehenge or the soaring vaults of Chartres or the ceiling of the Sistine Chapel; back then the scriptures were among mankind's greatest works of sacred art, meant to improve more than to prove, to evoke more than to evince, to unbind more than to bind. Back then people weren't so afraid of living within the Mystery.

I chose the Great Speckled Bird as the totem of this book simply because we cannot know what it is. It is what Rudolph Otto called the *mysterium tremendum*. It could be demon or angel, life or death, Creator or creature. And yet, life at its fullest is lived daily under its great soaring shadow with a feeling of awe in the chest, breath in the lungs, clearness in the head, exhilaration in the heart, and alertness in every muscle, tendon and cell of the body. That is what living with the Great Speckled Bird can do for you, if you are willing.

COMING HOME

I was not always a preacher. I fought the undertow of the family trade until midlife. But there were always times of going out to the foggy straits between earth and heaven, where the tides are ferocious and the water icy cold, and trying to make my way across at low tide, or occasionally, even on the flood, as preachers will try to do.

For a while I was a handyman around Concord, Massachusetts. One day I took a chimney sweeping job up on Nashawtuc Hill. The house, a grand three-story brick Tudor with slate roof, lightning rods and tall chimneys, belonged to a Democratic congresswoman.

"David," I said to my partner as we got out of our trucks and stared up at the chimney-tops, "this has got to be the biggest house we've ever done. You want up or down?" He shrugged, so we did rock-paper-scissors. He got the fireplace and I got the chimney top. I clambered up the big ladder onto the roof, scrambled up the slick slate, and began to walk the high ridge with my brushes on my back, holding a small ladder for balance like a high-wire act. I stepped safely over the tall lightning rods as I went, until I came to the last one.

Impaled on the cold iron spike was the spread-eagled, mummified body of a gray squirrel. His eye sockets were empty; his skin stretched and pale, his toes curled tight, his body rigid and brittle. Suddenly I felt kettle drums booming in my chest and the cold fingers of fear tightening around my throat. I stepped over the dead squirrel and kept walking until I could lean my ladder against the chimney and start climbing again. Today, no one would do this sort of work without a hydraulic lift or at least safety ropes and harness, but I climbed un-tethered to the top of the tall chimney and perched there listening to my heart pound and looking at the serene steeple of the Trinitarian Church by the milldam half a mile away.

"Dave," I called down the chimney as I sat there sweating and trembling in the November chill, "I'm up here."

"Good," came back a little voice from down in the dark tunnel, "Send the brush down." We scrubbed the brush up and down inside the chimney as clouds of black soot came up with the draft and showered down onto David. When we were done and it was time to come down, I froze.

"David," I called down, "I can't move!"

"You have to," piped up the distant voice. "Nobody but the fire department could get you down from there, and we can't call them. They recommended us for the job!" Knowing he was right, I moved. Very slowly. So slowly that it took about five years of my precious and dwindling youth to get back down onto the ground.

For a while I was the sexton of the Trinitarian Church. I scrubbed toilets, cleaned floors and windows, shoveled snow, and in between read most of the American Indian collection from the Concord Public Library while hidden in my office in the boiler room. I worked as a tree man, a custodian, a caretaker, a house painter, a teacher, and a musician.

For several years I was the foreman of a large commercial orchard in Worcester County. To provide a home and livelihood for my family, I single-handedly poisoned myriads of perfect insects, and will undoubtedly stand before the throne of the Great Grasshopper one day to answer for that. With a crew of from one to twenty, I directed all the pruning, mowing, cutting down old trees and planting new ones, and general care for a hundred acres of apple trees. My wife Becky and I and our two children lived in a house belonging to the farm.

Each year during the late summer and early fall, I was 'boss' to a crew of Jamaican migrant laborers who laughed and sang in the trees, and picked the ripe Cortland, Macintosh, and Delicious apples into their picking buckets to be tenderly emptied into 14-bushel bins. With a fork lift on the front of a John Deere 2240, I loaded the bins onto trailers to be trundled down to the packing house where a dozen local ladies sorted and packed them. I guess I've still spent as much time on a tractor or working with a chain-saw as I have delivering sermons.

One September during the picking the wealthy Boston Brahmin owner of the orchard called me in. He'd once said to me, "If all the apples fell from all the trees it wouldn't bother me: I wouldn't so much as miss my breakfast."

This day he said, "The Jamaicans are taking it too damned easy; I want you to lean harder on them." He looked at me with pale, steely eyes. "I want them to heap the bins." This meant adding two or three extra bushels to each bin. This also meant that the grower would get 17 bushels and pay the Jamaicans for 14.

When I told the workers, one of the older men, Uriel Godfrey, threw down his picking bucket. "We cannot do this: this is slavery!" he shouted with flashing eyes. Next day the men stayed in their bunkhouse refusing to pick, and I stayed with them. The owner was furious.

Next morning, a Sunday, I got a call from the owner. "You're done," he said. That evening, the Jamaicans came to our house. We all sang and they quoted Psalm 37 from memory: "Fret not your self for the wicked, for they will soon fade like the grass." They said, "Do not worry. One gate closes, another opens." Soon the local police chief came by with an eviction notice and we were homeless and jobless with winter coming on and no orchard work anywhere.

There was nothing left to do.

That's when I became a preacher.

The voice you will hear in these pages will echo the voice of my late father who was a preacher too, born and raised in the snow country of northern Japan, third and only surviving son of missionaries, and a descendant of wild Scots-Irish Holiness Methodists. It also echoes the voice of my late mother raised in a small town in Massachusetts, a descendant of proper Yankee Puritans. She was ordained with my father in Roundup, Montana in 1938, and saw all four of her children off to college and seminary. She was a gentle but firm feminist in the pulpit and out.

My paternal ancestor, Robert McCall, came to America from Northern Ireland in 1775. There he had been a weaver who wove a coverlet for the British king with an American eagle motif. George III somehow took this as an insult, and demanded my ancestor's head, so the story goes. This Robert McCall joined the Continental Army and fought at Saratoga and Yorktown. I have reason to think he might have visited Blue Hill in 1799 or thereabouts as a Methodist circuit rider. My mother's people came over on the *Arbella* with John Winthrop, and were Yankee Congregationalists since 1630.

In these pages you will also hear the voice of Rebecca Haley McCall, my partner of more than 40 years, whose passionate *Leo* fire for justice gets my lukewarm *Pisces* water steamed up as needed, and saves me from being one of God's frozen people. Her compassion has kept my heart alive, and her love and humor have preserved my sanity when all else was lost. Knowing her has made me whole, not as I imagined I needed to be, but as the Universe knew I needed to be. A marriage is a bit like a small town; the longer you live in it, the more you learn about it and love it.

I am no saint, no theologian, no prophet, and no expert on anything other than my own commonplace experiences. I have rarely heard the voice of God or of angels, nor ever been to the Holy Land. I yearn for no assurances of heaven. But I have been ever so surely guided, and have lived in this village with my wife and children and a truly inspired congregation long enough to know what heaven might be. If this sounds like rank sentimentality to you, maybe you should come to one of the world's countless surviving villages and see for yourself.

LOCAL HISTORY

In 1986 when we moved into the Theodore Stevens House in Blue Hill which is the parsonage for the Congregational Church, we found a number of relics from former times that were passed down from one occupant family to the next through the years. These included photographs, fireplace tools probably made by Stevens, and several pieces of furniture including dressers, a white marble-topped table, and a large glass-fronted Ruskin bookcase. In that bookcase I found an ancient leather-bound book, entitled *Discourse Concerning the Holy Spirit*, by John D Owen DD. It has numerous hand-written annotations throughout and slips of paper and dried flowers pressed between its pages. I have inscribed it myself, made minor repairs on it, read in it (as much as my sorely limited tolerance for Calvinistic theology would allow), and added other local samples to the pressed flowers over the years.

This particular volume has an interesting history, to say the least. It was published in London in 1676. The author John Owen DD (1616-1683) was a Puritan, chaplain of the Long Parliament, and a Congregationalist. Owen wrote many books on Calvinist theology and we know that Jonathan Fisher (1768-1847), first settled minister in Blue Hill, studied Owen because he notes in his journal several times that he "read in Owen" (usually on a Sunday marked with a dominical letter).

The name *Joshua Gee 1725* is inscribed on the title page of the book. This inscription was later covered over with circular scribbles. Joshua Gee 1698-1748 was a prominent Congregationalist minister in Boston who delivered a celebrated eulogy for Cotton Mather's funeral, called "Israel's Mourning for Aaron's Death," in 1728.

On the title page also are inscribed the words *Bathsheba Savage from her friend Samuel Ph Savage*. The words *Samuel Ph Savage bought at vendue 1773* are inscribed on the second page. The second 7 in the date looks like a 9 but is probably not because Bathsheba Savage died in 1792. The Savage family is descended from Thomas Savage (1608-1682), who emigrated from England to Boston in 1635. Samuel Phillips Savage, his great-grandson, insured vessels and cargo in Boston's shipping business and lived in Weston, Massachusetts. He was an active patriot who was president of the Massachusetts Board of War and took part in the Boston Tea Party. Samuel Phillips Savage's first wife, Sarah Tyler, died in February of 1764; his second wife, Bathsheba, in June of 1792.

The inscription *Rev E. Bean Gray Maine 1890* appears on the inside of the front cover and also on a pasted-in piece of lined paper. According to Blake's history *Two Hundred Years*, Ebenezer Bean 1809(?)-1910 became the pastor of the Blue Hill Congregational Church in 1893.

The words *Samuel W. Emery Portland Maine* are inscribed vertically on the inside front cover. I can find no information about Emery.

On the top center inside front cover there is a pasted label which is printed across the top "OTIS LITTLEFIELD, M.D.

BLUEHILL, MAINE." On the label is hand written, *Given to me 1910 by Ebenezer Bean, Pastor Congo Church. Died Walnut Hill 101 years old Book date 1676* Doctor Littlefield is still remembered around here as a beloved family doctor and one of the founders of the Blue Hill Hospital.

Imagine my astonishment when some time ago I opened the book and found that Dr. Littlefield's label had fallen off to show the inscription *Jon. Fisher from Rob't. McCall.* If my memory serves, Fisher noted in his journal for August of 1799, "attended lecture by Mr. McCall." Midweek lectures were usually delivered by clergy who were designated "Rev." This lecture, however, was different, and leads to the following wild speculation.

As mentioned earlier, my direct ancestor, Robert McCall, was a weaver. Family legend says that he wove a bedspread for George III with an American eagle design. The king was not pleased and put a price on his head. He fled from Ireland to America in 1775, fought at Saratoga and Yorktown and became a Wesleyan circuit rider after the war. These worthies traveled far and wide to preach, and were not referred to as "Rev." but as "Mr."

Perhaps my ancestor over 200 years ago came to Blue Hill, walked the same byways that I walk, and gave this book to Jonathan Fisher. Or perhaps there is another explanation for this remarkable coincidence. Either way, it is easy to see why I find the history of this singular volume to be fascinating. It has passed through some very interesting hands in its 340 years and is well worth preserving as a significant historical document of our nation, town, and church, and as a symbol of the continuing marvels and mysteries of life in Blue Hill

Our congregation was first gathered in Blue Hill, Maine in 1772. Visitors often say, "What do you do in such a little town all winter? Who do you talk to?" What do we do? In winter we do everything we do in summer, and then we also haul wood for the stoves, shovel snow, take off coats and boots and put them on again, look out for each other, and celebrate the holidays and the joy of living. There's always plenty to do. Whom do we talk to? We talk to each other, the chickadees and cedar waxwings, the trees, the mountain, the storms, and the Lord of Storms. There's always someone to talk to. And, winter, spring, summer and fall, I write about all these things.

Jonathan Fisher graduated from Harvard in 1796 and came to Maine with his wife, Dolly. He served the church for over 40 years, as was typical in those days. He saw the holy in both scripture and Nature.

Fisher built his own house, made his own tools and furniture, raised his own food, made medicines from local plants, carved wood-cuts of the animals mentioned in the Bible, kept a journal of his activities for over 30 years, published numerous volumes, and painted four portraits of himself, though (for reasons open to speculation) none of any other family member. His earnest, centered, and sometimes narrow rigor is characteristic of preachers, as may be evidenced by the volume you hold in your hand.

During the time that Jonathan Fisher served the Blue Hill Church, he often walked the 35 miles to Bangor for meetings at the Seminary which he helped to found. We've done that too. He also walked the 160 or more miles to St. Andrews, New Brunswick and back on missionary tours, helping to start several churches in deepest Washington County. We haven't done that yet.

Fisher's house in Blue Hill has been restored and is now the temple of the Fisher Society which reveres his memory. I will not say that there is a Jonathan Fisher cult in Blue Hill, but there are relics, sacred books, and maybe now and then a big Buick with a blue-haired lady behind the wheel and a little plastic statue of Fisher on the dashboard.

In Jonathan Fisher's time, the vocation of ministry was considered one of the highest a person could attain, far above politics, and equal to medicine and law. Ministers were among the most educated and influential members of the community, and many college graduates went into ministry. I remember Prof. Doug Walrath at Bangor Seminary remarking that in those days a preacher might be expected to serve one church for life. Some served two. Those who served more were considered the ne'er-do-wells.

In the 1960s and '70s the work of small-town ministry began to lose its luster. Many clergy became infected with the virus of success, which caused them to stay for a short time and then move to a larger, more prestigious church which paid more. One local, on hearing that his minister had gone on to a richer pulpit, put it this way: "The Rev'rent," he said, "has heard the call."

During those years many small churches dwindled and died, and college graduates increasingly went into teaching, business and law. The excesses of televangelists and the rise of mega-churches in the 1980s and '90s served to further discourage promising students from going into small church ministry. Small churches = small potatoes.

By this time, you may have discovered that your author has a raging bias in favor of small towns and churches. I cannot disguise it, nor do I wish to. Part of my intention is to sway you, too, and perhaps call you to a richer and simpler way of life.

Today, countless small towns and churches have the benefit of being closer to the culture of the land, which until the last century was the culture of most of the human race. Many small churches are still grounded in the original natural environment of forests, fields, and agricultural activities, and as Wendell Berry says, "All culture is agriculture." This grounding is echoed in the Bible's earthy imagery for wisdom, faith and a righteous life.

Urban and suburban churches, by contrast, often adopt business models and language, and judge their success by the 'bottom line.' Their goals may become getting more members and more income. When this happens, they cease being Biblical and become commercial. This creates a deep disconnection with the life of the spirit. Likewise, larger churches may adopt the language of secular psychology emphasizing the therapeutic redemption of the individual through happiness or well-being. This also creates a disconnection with the full life of the Spirit.

The commercial and psychological models are dangerous for churches for many reasons, but primarily because they lose their grounding in the Spirit. These models substitute matter or mind for spirit as the center of the redeemed life. They divide the person and the world into pieces and create specialists. You go to the car wash to wash your car, and you go to church to cleanse your soul. But the human person is an organism made of indivisible parts.

As in any living body, when the parts are divided from each other, the Spirit flees. The small church is not a business or a spa or mental health clinic. If it tries to be these things, it fails. That is because the small church is not a mechanism. It is an organic being, a living organism with a soul, grounded in a whole living community.

This grounding echoes biblical teachings about the vineyard, the flock, the fish of the sea, the beasts of the field and the birds of the air describing the healthy life of the spirit. All of these are ecological communities dependent upon the well-being of other living communities. In such interdependent communities, the ill health of one part threatens the good health of the whole. The lesson here is that there can be no individual salvation apart from the whole. The self is the enemy of salvation more than its subject. The one who would save himself, must lose himself in the whole. That is the meaning of 'holy.'

American Christianity has become obsessed with individual salvation through the 'blood atonement,' which declares that the brutal suffering and death of Christ is the only means of our salvation. This strange doctrine is far from central to Christ's teaching, appearing in only a few places in the Gospels. Perhaps because of our bloody national history, this obsession has grown more and more pervasive from the time of Jonathan Edwards to Charles Finney to Billy Sunday to Billy Graham to Pat Robertson at a rate roughly comparable to the movement of the population away from country to city, and in proportion to the numbers who have died in our wars.

Today blood atonement has become a demon demanding proof of salvation for the self-chosen people built on the blood and suffering of the weak and powerless. As a result, churches have offered increasingly simplistic guarantees of something that is entirely beyond their knowledge and out of their hands.

Believers are assured that a few magic words will force the hand of the Creator of the Universe in their favor. If we utter the magic words, we can be Raptured into Heaven when things get tough, and it's to Hell with the poor fools that didn't get the message. Or we can turn God into a vending machine that will give us the jackpot if we say the right words. This is the opposite of faith. Faith is trusting in God to do the right thing, not manipulating the deity by quick formulas torn away from the whole fabric of scripture, like John 3:16.

My father used to say, "There is no fight like a church fight," and he was right. When Christians take the gloves off, look out. In the early 80s the Blue Hill church, like many others, was torn asunder by a nasty battle between evangelicals and liberals. This conflict resulted in the dismissal of a minister under very trying circumstances. An interim minister helped to get the church back on its feet. It was into this situation that we arrived in Blue Hill in the fall of 1986 when I was 42 and still very green at the preacher's trade.

In the past 25 years our church has changed, but it has not gotten much bigger in number. We have welcomed about as many new members as we have buried: around 200. We have seen 200 or so children come up through our Sunday School. We have also seen 10 church members go into ministry themselves.

We have soldiered through numerous capital campaigns, over a thousand coffee hours with untold thousands of cookies and vegetable dips, bowls of turquoise punch, and coffee that would take the rust off the bumper of your car. We have held thousands of meetings on folding chairs under old fluorescent lights. I have preached roughly a thousand sermons, or, as some might say, one sermon a thousand times.

Preaching is an art more than a science, and good preaching is about listening as much as talking. If the preacher isn't hearing the congregation every day of the week, the congregation is not going to hear the preacher on Sunday morning. Good preaching speaks to the soul: the soul being, not a thing, but the marriage of the spirit and the flesh moving together, singing together.

People have souls. Churches do too. The preacher needs to know that. This does not mean that the preacher is always going to say exactly what the congregation wants to hear. Sometimes the preacher will want to say exactly what they want to hear; but to speak to the soul, sometimes the preacher had better say exactly what they don't want to hear.

Like scripture, the following pages are both fact and fantasy. Both have their purposes. If you would find any truth herein, I beg you to read not with your head alone but with your heart also, not literally but poetically. In the following entries I use various names for God. All have their limitations. I am not sure whether I am a deist, a theist, a pantheist, an atheist or an agnostic. Some days I'm one; some days I'm another. It doesn't matter anymore.

I *am* sure that there is a Spirit in the universe that still and always moves from nothing to something, from chaos to order, from brokenness to healing, from dissonance to harmony, from ugliness to elegance, from hatred to love, and from yesterday to tomorrow. This Spirit also moves me, sometimes methodically, sometimes ecstatically.

The selected almanacs were previously published in local papers and elsewhere. The journals and letters are previously unpublished. I have changed names to protect privacy when that seemed warranted. The sermons were preached from the Bible to a peerless, imperfect, living congregation over the course of many years. All entries were written through war and peace, good times and bad, storms and calms, tragedies and triumphs; but for the most part during our government's wars in Iraq and Afghanistan and during an era when the divide between rich and poor was growing ever more severe and the lust for money was corrupting our national soul and our institutions. Entries are roughly organized through the seasons, beginning with Spring, because that is when life begins around here.

Spring

Spring

MARCH

March's warm days and cold nights are starting the sap to running at last. Cardinals, crows and gulls call brightly at dawn. Choruses of starlings gather in the tree-tops. Red squirrels are active again after a couple of months of rest. The ice is still thick in the harbor as great frozen ledges push up against each other at low tide, then settle out flat, squeaking and groaning as the tide comes back in.

Warmer days bring out walkers along the roads. I started walking up Pleasant Street toward the Mountain Road on the way to pick up my truck at Bowden's garage the other day. I was making pretty good time up the hill, I thought. I stopped for just a moment to watch some mourning doves flirting in the trees and noticed a woman coming up the hill far behind me. "I'll show her," I said to myself, and started up again at a brisk pace, not wanting to be overtaken.

Far sooner than I expected, I heard footsteps right behind me. "Holy Crow!" I thought, "She's really moving." I stepped aside just in time to be passed by none other than Leslie Clapp, probably Blue Hill's preeminent walker. Leslie has walked the entire Appalachian Trail, the entire Pacific Crest Trail, and—who knows—maybe the Oregon Trail, too. I was honored, and humbled, as she disappeared in the distance.

March also means town meeting, one of the oldest forms of grassroots democracy anywhere, stemming from the ancient tribal council of our ancestors, and the congregational meeting. Every adult citizen can vote. We elect our leaders from selectmen to road commissioner to tree warden to overseer of the poor. In New England, town meeting government is older than state and federal governments; and I imagine if our federal and state governments were to collapse tomorrow (as if they hadn't already), we would not falter or fail. We would quickly gather and laboriously and loquaciously figure out what to do next. Why? Because we have been practicing this ancient and honorable administration of our own affairs since the first Europeans set foot on American soil. But there are serious problems with town meeting government today.

Too many citizens, who day after day rant along with talk-radio pundits about corrupt politicians and the abuse of the common man, somehow can't make it down to the town hall or the school gym just once a year to exercise their right to speak and vote. Towns far and wide are giving up on town meeting altogether with hardly a whimper. It's a crying shame. In Blue Hill we're lucky to get more than one out of ten voters to show up for this elegant exercise in grassroots government. Some complain that a small special interest group can sway a town meeting. True, but that can only happen when the population at large does not turn out. Our freedoms cannot be taken away without our consent. Silence is consent.

EASTER

Every Easter we have a sunrise service on the mountain looking over towards Mt. Cadillac. Some years the full moon is setting behind us while the sun is rising before us. It's breath-taking. If it's snowing we meet in the church. For over 50 years we have done this jointly with the Baptists. Both churches take turns putting on a hearty cardiac breakfast with sausage, bacon, eggs, muffins, homemade donuts, and everything.

One old fellow didn't like church so much as he liked breakfast. One year the Congregationalists departed from tradition and served quiche. The poor fellow took one look at it, stood up and barked, "Where's my G__ d___ breakfast?" and walked out.

Easter morning the regulars try to get there early to sit in their favorite pew because the church fills right up. Some grumble about the "Creasters" who come only on Christmas and Easter. I don't care, just so long as they come. People look forward to Easter around here because Winter can be long and rough. So, when we're singing "Hallelujah! The strife is o'er the battle won," believe me, it's heartfelt.

Most people I talk to these days are far more concerned about the Passion of the Earth than the Passion of Christ, but the two are really the same drama, the same Passion Play. Like Judas, we have betrayed them both. Like Peter, we have denied them. Both have been brutalized and abused. Too often the Right talks about God and ignores Nature, while the Left talks about Nature and ignores God. But the two are one: Nature is the body, and God is the soul of the Cosmos.

Last week I talked with a local organic farmer/carpenter, a good man who was seriously grieving the death of coral reefs as a result of the warming of the oceans. His grief was very much like what many are feeling about the world. The huge BP gusher in the Gulf of Mexico might as well have been pumping sludge into our veins. It is making us all sick with grief. Maybe you remember the iconic *Time* cover story about global warming with a picture of a lonely polar bear on an ice flow under huge bold letters: BE WORRIED. BE VERY, VERY WORRIED! I got a sick feeling just looking at it. But then I said to myself, "Wait Rob, this is not a message from God. This is a message from Time/Warner."

What was the message of the Psalms? Was it to be very, very worried? No. It was "God is our refuge and strength a very present help in trouble. Therefore we shall not fear though the earth should change."

What was the message of the angels over Bethlehem? Was it, "Be Very Worried?" No. It was, "Fear not, for we bring good news of great joy that will be to all people."

What was the message from the angel to the three Marys at the empty tomb when they found the stone rolled away? Was it to worry? No. It was, "Fear not, I know you seek the crucified Jesus, but he is not here. He is risen."

The changes we are seeing in the environment show once again the reality of a higher order to the Cosmos than the whims of mankind. Our teachers and prophets were absolutely right. We reap what we sow. If we follow only our own plans and appetites, we bring harm to the Holy Body of Nature. By the same token, if we follow the laws of Nature and Nature's God, we bring healing. If we can hurt the Creation then, by God, we can heal it.

Oil billionaire J. Paul Getty once said, "The meek will inherit the earth, but not until I'm done with it." Well, he and his kind are done with it, and the meek stand ready to take over. When the people lead, the leaders will follow. "Don't mourn, boys," said Joe Hill, "Organize." There are manifest signs that left and right, red and blue are coming together to heal the One Holy Body. Remember Margaret Mead: "Never doubt that a small group of concerned people can change the world. Indeed, nothing else ever has."

I'm going to interrupt the sacred drama of Easter for a moment with a sermon:

"It is a great joy for this preacher to look out over the congregation and see you all here. The Noah family and all the animals might have felt a little bit like this after the ark settled down on dry ground. There is a definite mood of survival here today. It is not as though this was a particularly rough winter. It wasn't. But we have survived much more than just winter. We have survived some sadness and sorrow. We have survived the swine flu and the winter cold and the politics of pugnacity. We have survived the slings and arrows of outrageous fortune. We have survived crossing the street, crossing the country and crossing the world. And we have survived living day to day with those we care about, which is no small task.

"We have survived loss and change too. When we close our eyes for a prayer, it seems things look a certain way and certain dear people are near us. When we open our eyes again, things have changed and new people are there, the ones we knew are gone. We remember them today at this wrinkle in sacred time.

"By coming here we are part of something much greater than we can imagine—a story much greater than any one person's story—and we revel in it and are lifted up and carried away by it. We are made more real by it. It is a Mystery Play because our knowledge about where we come from and where we go reaches only a little farther than our hands can reach. Our knowledge is bounded and limited. Life begins and ends in mystery and we could beat our brains out trying to set down all the answers. Instead, we come here to take part in the great Mystery Play, for the wonder of it and for the joy and comfort of being in it together. We sit next to each other singing and praying our little hearts out through despair, sickness, sorrow, loneliness, death resurrection, birth, life, joy and even ecstasy, while the Creator of All Mystery goes on before us in a cloud of unknowing."

There was a time when we thought the mystery was way out there somewhere at the far edge of our knowledge and retreating fast at the onslaught of our marvelous intellect like the fog before a North wind. We even thought the Mystery would disappear altogether some time soon, wiped out by our intelligence. But we began to notice the Great Mystery slipping back in around us like a gentle mist, creeping in, surrounding us. We read the paper and watch the news and shake our heads at the mysteries which have developed a resistance to our knowledge and are multiplying and abounding.

There was a time when we had it all down in a pat set of beliefs printed in the back of the hymnal or the prayer-book or on a page in the church by-laws: We believe this and we believe that, etc. etc... But we don't agree on that anymore—probably never did really—and even if we did it would fill volumes. So awkwardly enough, maybe we are not sure what to believe.

Not sure what to believe'? Isn't that just awful? Isn't that just another sign of wishy-washy liberalism and the decadence and breakdown of modern western civilization?

I'll give you one person's answer: I don't care what you believe, frankly. Without trying to be too blunt about it, I don't care if you believe that Christ was actually bodily resurrected from the condition of being clinically dead, or if you believe it's all a bunch of hooey.

I don't care what you believe. I care what you love. If you love the Creator and your neighbor and yourself and your family and your dog and your enemy and the Earth and the Great Mystery, then what in the world do you need beliefs for? And if you don't love these things, what earthly good will beliefs do you anyway? We are what we love far more than we are what we believe. All the beliefs in the world in all the ages of time cannot embrace the Mystery, while love can embrace it effortlessly in the twinkling of an eye. Mysteries are revealed unto the meek. They don't need any Giant Hadron Collider.

That is what we're doing here, if you ask me, embracing the Mystery. We try to love each other, through the cloud of unknowing, with God going on before us.

That is where we are...
At the end of Winter,
At the beginning of Spring,
In this Mystery Play of birth, life, death and resurrection.
Now, on with the play.

PRUNING

The recent warmer weather draws this old tree man irresistibly away from his endless paper-work and outside to prune the apple trees of which he has about a dozen in his care. Pruning out the top of an ancient standard Wolf River apple tree we've pruned every year for the last 23 years 18-20 feet up in the Spring air with the sun shining, the warming ground giving off its earthy perfume, and the gulls and turkey vultures wheeling overhead, makes the winter-weary heart swell nearly to bursting with joy and contentment. Hand and eye and pruning saw work together out of habit, leaving the mind free to wander where it will.

Some philosophers will argue that we cannot look for moral values in Nature, leaving this poor philosopher to ask, "Where else are we to look, for pity's sake?" The philosopher is Nature. The apple tree is Nature; the ground is Nature. So are the birds and the sky and the man doing the pruning: Nature feeding Nature, Nature eating Nature, Nature tending Nature, Nature contemplating Nature.

The ancients saw that what we call "ecosystems" or the "biosphere" are like a tree. They called it, truly enough, the Tree of

Life. This tree appears in countless ancient myths and in the first and last books of the Bible—Genesis and Revelation. Charles Darwin used the image of a tree to describe natural selection. Anthropologists use the image of the tree to describe human evolution. Your commentator sees the mutual care-taking between apple trees and humans as a model for the best of human culture. The human keeps the tree healthy and fruitful and the apple tree reciprocates.

The apple tree depends on the earth for nurture and support, on water for moisture, on the air for respiration, and on the sun for the light and heat to make food. If any of these is polluted or diminished, the tree will suffer. No moral lessons here?

Branches going straight up grow too fast, are bright and fresh, showy and leafy, but take more than their share of energy and tend to over-top and dominate the tree. They are also soft and weak, and bear no fruit. So the careful pruner cuts them off. Slower growing branches grow not upward, but outward, and bear more fruit. Branches growing downward are also pruned off. So are dead branches. No moral lesson?

Furthermore, thick, rank branches too close together discourage growth of fruit and encourage disease. So, the careful pruner cuts out thick and tangled branches to keep the whole tree open to the free movement of air and the blessing of sunlight. If the roots are damaged and unable to do their work, the tree suffers and may die. But, if the tree is damaged, as long as the roots are strong, the tree will regenerate. No moral lessons here?

True or false, here are the moral lessons the orchard philosopher takes from the apple tree. It does not go well for the Tree of Life when there is too much fast and showy upward growth, for this takes too much from the rest of the tree and is not fruitful. It does not go well when the roots are not healthy, for then the whole tree suffers. It does not go well for the Tree of Life when its growth is tangled and rank, for then light and air cannot move freely through the tree to keep it healthy.

It goes well for the Tree of Life when the earth, the air and the water are healthy, for then the roots and the whole tree will be strong. It goes well for the Tree of Life when the upward growth which seeks to dominate is pruned off. It goes well when the more fruitful wood is favored, and the less fruitful is cut out. It goes well when there is free movement of light and air throughout the tree.

It goes well when—as it was in the beginning, is now and ever shall be—the Great Cosmic Pruner wields the pruning saw for the sake of the whole Tree of Life to cut out what grows too fast, or is overbearing and unfruitful, and favors what grows slowly and bears good fruit. And even if the tree is broken by wind or burned by fire or lightning, as long as the roots are healthy, it will rise again.

Are there no moral lessons here?

PENTECOST

In ancient times the whole cosmos and everything in it were understood to be composed of certain fundamental elements. In the West, these elements were earth, water, wind and fire. Of these elements everything was made, and to these elements everything returned. Human beings were made of these elements too. Our flesh and bone came from earth; our blood, sweat and tears came from water. These are the material elements. Human breath came from air; and energy or vitality from fire. These are the spiritual elements. When the elements come together there is life. When the breath and fire leave the body, when the spiritual is separated from the material, death is the result, or so it was understood by the ancients.

In Hebrew, Latin and Greek we find that the words for "Spirit" and "Breath" are the same. In Hebrew the word is "Ruach." In Greek it is "Pneuma:" air, lungs, breath. In Latin the root is "Spir-" from which we get *spirit, aspire, inspiration, respiration,* and so forth. Everything that has breath has spirit. In Hebrew and Greek, by the way, the word for spirit is a *feminine* noun. In Latin it is masculine, which might explain some things... like celibacy and patriarchy.

Beginning in the 4th century B.C. the ancient elements began to lose their symbolic power in the West. Greek philosophers like Democritus pursued a materialistic physics seeking that irreducible bit of spirit-less matter that was the basic building block of the whole universe. These philosophers rejected the fundamental elements of earth, air, fire and water as primitive and unsophisticated. This rejection is remarkably similar to the current animosity between Darwinists and Creationists. The one has no need for spirit to explain the universe and the other is adamant that spirit is of the essence.

By any measure, materialistic views of the universe have proven successful in many ways through centuries. They have explained the movement and composition of everything from atomic particles to galaxies. The Periodical Table of the Elements which we struggled with in high school is the direct descendant of the atomists, and chemistry has allowed us to harness the primordial power of the atom for good or ill.

But today the materialistic view of the cosmos may have reached its limits in physics, and in the human soul. In modern materialistic physics the atom, once thought to be irreducible, has been broken down into many ever smaller particles, some of which do not act like matter at all, but more like energy. Einstein showed that matter is, in the end, a form of energy. Furthermore, the materialistic and anti-spiritual world-view in the 20th century presided over the death of millions of souls in the atrocities of two World Wars, the Holocaust, Hiroshima, Nagasaki and the brutality of Stalin and Mao. When the Spirit departs, Death rules.

On the day of Pentecost the followers of Jesus were gathered in a house in Jerusalem waiting and wondering what to do. The Father, God, seemed very far away. The Son, Jesus Christ, had been taken up into heaven to sit on the right hand of the Father. The disciples were feeling alone, dispirited, uninspired, holding their breath. "Suddenly," writes Luke, "a sound came from heaven like the rush of a mighty wind and it filled the house where they were sitting. And there appeared to them tongues as of fire resting on each one of them. And they were all filled with the Spirit and began to speak in other tongues."

As they waited there, the spirit-less material elements of their bodies—earth and water—were suddenly filled with the spiritual elements—wind and fire. The Spirit rushed in and they were inspired and revived. A new living body was formed from them: Matter was again filled with Spirit. Pentecost marked the movement of the Holy Spirit from Christ himself into his followers, from the one to the many.

Spirit now resided no longer in the departed leader, but in the activity of the whole community, a new holy body. The Buddhists call it "Sangha." The Jews call it "Torah." Christians call it "Ecclesia;" another feminine name, by the way. The Spirit gave birth to the church and, appropriately enough, they are both called "She." Let's never forget that.

And we are gathered here in that kind of primitive church. We can comprehend and accept and work with modern chemistry and the periodic table of the elements just fine, yet we also live in the ancient alchemy of the primal elements. How so?

We simply do not accept that the universe is composed of nothing but soul-less matter.

We do not accept that people, plants, animals, and elements are nothing but material things to be used.

We do not accept that the land and everything in it are nothing but material commodities to be bought and sold.

We see the material world as breathing and glowing with unquenchable spirit.

And we know that the Spirit is present here when we gather. We know it because we feel it.

A VERY OLD STORY

*This piece was written during the
"Shock & Awe" bombing of Baghdad.*

Here is an old story: Long ago there were many kingdoms. Some were rich and powerful. Others were poor and weak. Some were ruled by good kings who took care of their own people and their neighbors. Others were ruled by wicked kings who abused their people and attacked their neighbors. Now and then, a powerful kingdom with a wicked king would make war upon its neighbors causing great suffering, most especially among women and children who wanted nothing more than to live their lives in peace.

In those days, one or another powerful kingdom would begin to believe that it could conquer the whole world and would set out to do so, with no thought to the suffering it might cause. For a time some powerful kingdom might subdue others by force of arms, and for a time, the world would be without war. Yet, the many conquered lived in slavery, suffering, deprivation, hunger and poverty while the conqueror prospered.

Time and again, the great and powerful conquering kingdom

after a while would fall of its own weight, and yet another kingdom would rise to power and seek to enslave the others. This
cruel pattern continued for thousands of years. After a particularly horrible war when millions died and millions more were
left devastated and homeless, some wise leaders began to dream
about ending this horrible and inhuman pattern.

They agreed to form a council in which representatives from
all countries would gather to handle conflicts that might arise
between them. They agreed upon a bill of rights for all people,
from kings to peasants. They outlawed slavery, torture, genocide,
and attacks upon one nation by another. They set up a high court
to rule upon abuses of those rights and to settle conflicts between
kingdoms. They even provided for a corps of men and women
from every kingdom to keep the peace between kingdoms.

Still, for a time, one powerful kingdom or another would ignore
the voice of all the others and set out for its own ends to conquer
the world as in former days. Each time this happened the suffering
was greater, especially on the women and children. And each time,
the great and mighty conqueror at last would fall of its own weight
as before, and the bigger they were, the harder they fell. Others
were left to pick up the pieces, to help the hungry and the homeless, to fight poverty and disease, to foster learning and peace.

At last, all the kingdoms began to see that war and violence,
poverty and ignorance were simply diseases like smallpox and
yellow fever, and that the cure was available, if only they would
labor together to bring it about. And so, they did. It did not happen overnight. Just like the overcoming of other human diseases,
it took the faithful struggle and sacrifice of many people for many
years. But, at last the whole world came into a time when swords
were beaten into plowshares and spears into pruning hooks,
when all the boots of the tramping warriors and all the chariots
of war were burned with fire, when children were no longer born
to calamity, and every man beneath his vine and fig tree could live
in peace and unafraid. Wasn't that a time?

41

It was. And, isn't this the most ancient and deep desire of human hearts since the beginning? It is. Isn't this a wonderful story? It is, but it isn't over yet.

And, is this a true story, or a fancy fable?

Well, now that would be up to all of us.

MOTHER'S DAY

Will Rogers used to say that Mother's Day was "the one day we give to our mothers while they give us the other 364. We all go over to Mother's to tell her how much we love her while she cooks a big dinner for us." Across the world, across the ages, and even across species, mother-love is a primordial power not to be trifled with.

The fierce maternal instinct of bears, for example, is legendary. A sow bear with cubs to defend is a formidable creature, to be avoided in the wild at all costs. You've probably heard the story about the two men who were confronted by a mother bear. One stopped to put on running shoes. The other shouted, "You'll never outrun that bear!" The first shouted back, "I only have to outrun you!" There was even a story in the *Bangor Daily* some time ago of a mother bear taking in a wandering beagle pup and lavishing it with motherly affection until its owner found it and with some difficulty removed it from the bear's den.

It is my experience that humans are much the same. Mothers will go to extreme lengths of labor and self-sacrifice to protect the welfare of children. Unfortunately, in both species the paternal instinct is rarely so strong. Single mothers vastly outnumber single fathers. Women teachers, nurses, social workers, and caregivers greatly outnumber men. The human maternal instinct to protect the young from danger can be bear-like in its ferocity. But where is Poppa Bear?

One day last week a plainly dressed woman came meekly into the church looking for help. She had just enough gas in her rusty truck to get to work here in town, but no money and not enough gas to get back home. She was short on food with two children to feed and afraid she wasn't going to be able to pay the rent. Her husband walked out and lives in Bangor. He is not helping. We did what we could to help her and we prayed together. She left with tears running down her face.

But you know, of the 60 or so peninsula households with children or elderly we assist year after year, over 50 are headed by women. Nationwide, 12% of all households are headed by women with children. The percentage is far higher among poor households. In the wealthiest country in the world, some 40 million people, including 15 million children, face hunger; and that number is growing according to most reports. Somehow all the lovely sentiments about motherhood we hear this time of year ring hollow in the face of the stark realities that too many mothers face here and around the world every single day. It's enough to make you weep. Without caring fathers, though it may not thrive, the human race may survive. But without caring mothers, it cannot thrive, nor will it survive.

Year after year schools across the country struggle to make ends meet while our defense spending—nearly $1 trillion annually, almost as much as the combined defense budgets of every other country in the world—gets bigger and bigger and bigger. "It'll be a great day," says the bumper sticker, "when schools have all the money they need, and the Air Force has to hold bake sales to pay for a new bomber."

Modern war is a far greater danger to both mothers and

young of our species than it is to fathers for several reasons: First, because war burns up money and resources that ought to be improving the lives of children. Second, because civilian casualties—women and children—greatly exceed military casualties, as in our government's current follies in Iraq, Afghanistan, and now Pakistan (without any declaration of war). Third, for every soldier who dies there is at least a mother, and often a wife and children, left to pick up the broken pieces. Fathers have made war for thousands of years while mothers have mourned it with millions of tears. When the disease of war is finally eliminated from the earth, you can be sure that mothers will be in the forefront.

Julia Ward Howe is best known for her stirring Civil War hymn "The Battle Hymn of the Republic" which she wrote after the first battle of Bull Run in 1861 when many thought the war would end in a few weeks. Her hymn swept the country and still stirs the heart. But after watching four years of brutal war, waged with modern weapons but primitive medicine, leaving 2/3rds of a million dead and millions maimed, Julia Ward Howe had a profound change of heart. Having seen the horrors of that war and its aftermath, as well as the nearly 200,000 killed in the Franco Prussian War, in 1870 she published a national Mother's Day proclamation for peace:

Arise then...women of this day!
Arise, all women who have hearts!
Whether your baptism be of water or of tears!
Say firmly: "We will not have questions answered by
  irrelevant agencies,
Our husbands will not come to us, reeking with carnage,
For caresses and applause.
Our sons shall not be taken from us to unlearn
All that we have been able to teach them of charity,
  mercy and patience.
We, the women of one country,
Will be too tender of those of another country

To allow our sons to be trained to injure theirs."
From the bosom of a devastated Earth a voice goes up with
Our own. It says: "Disarm! Disarm!
The sword of murder is not the balance of justice."
Blood does not wipe out dishonor,
Nor violence indicate possession.
As men have often forsaken the plough and the anvil
At the summons of war,
Let women now leave all that may be left of home
For a great and earnest day of counsel...
Whereby the great human family can live in peace...

In the voice of Julia Ward Howe's stirring proclamation we can hear the voice of Mother Wisdom, a semi-divine figure known to nearly all ancient cultures. In some she is called "Sophia." She speaks in the eighth chapter of the Book of Proverbs, and this is what she says:

"Does not Wisdom call? At the entrance of the town she cries aloud: 'To you, O men, I call... O foolish men, pay attention. Hear, for I will speak noble things... Take my instruction rather than silver and knowledge better than choice gold. Pride and arrogance and the way of evil and twisted speech, I hate... The Lord created me at the beginning of his work, the first of his acts of old... and I was daily his delight, rejoicing before him always, rejoicing in his inhabited world and delighting in the sons of men. And now my sons, listen to me: happy are those who keep my ways... for he who finds me finds life, but he who misses me hurts himself; all who hate me love death'"

Jesus tells his followers to love one another. But you see, most mothers don't have to be told to love; they love by nature. Maybe that's why there were no women among the twelve disciples; they were already out there loving. Maybe that's why the Spanish proverb says, "An ounce of mother is worth a pound of priests." Maybe that is why the human race is still around.

We're going to have a Maypole after church. In early Christian times May Day was dedicated to Mother Mary. So, in closing I'm going to turn to Julian of Norwich, the great medieval mystic poet whose feast day was Friday, describing her mystical vision of Mary, so very like the young mother who wept in my office last week:

> *Then God brought our Lady into my mind, a meek and*
> *simple maid, young of age, in the same bodily form as when*
> *she conceived... With this sight I really understood that she is*
> *greater in worthiness and greatness than all*
> *God made below her... This little thing that is made... God*
> *showed it to me as small as if it had been a hazel-nut...*
> *I looked at it and thought, 'What can this be?' And the*
> *answer came to me, "It is all that is made.' I wondered how*
> *it could last, for it was so small I thought it might suddenly*
> *disappear. And the answer in my mind was, 'It lasts and*
> *will last forever because God loves it; and in the same way,*
> *everything exists through the love of God.'*

"This is my commandment, that you love one another, for love is of God."

SONS OF CARPENTERS

This is dedicated to my son Daniel McCall, carpenter, to my son-in-law Jonathan Wass, carpenter and cabinet-maker, and to all the wise and peaceful carpenters out there. All creatures have tools given them by Providence to make their living: the elephant's trunk, the raccoon's hands, the wolf's teeth, the crow's beak. Man calls himself the only tool-making animal, though research has shown that primates use rocks and sticks as tools, that the sea otter uses stones to crack oyster shells, and that some crows use straw to gather ants out of their nests. Still, man has reason to be proud of his success at making tools, as well as repentant of his failure to use the right tool for the right job.

"Give a man a hammer," goes the old saying, "and everything looks like a nail." On the job-site, when something won't open or close or go in or out, the cry soon goes up for the "Bigger Hammer." And certainly pounding is one of the first human skills to develop, as any parent of a two-year-old will tell you. Will Rogers brought this truth into the political arena when he remarked, "When the Congress is in session, everyone feels the way they do when the baby gets a-hold of a hammer." But we are not babies, nor should we act like them.

Our country's recent adventures in Iraq should prove to any doubters the danger of using the Big Hammer to get the job done when another tool would do less damage, a lesson that any mature and seasoned carpenter knows. Yes, Saddam Hussein used his Big Hammer ruthlessly, and great was the damage he inflicted. Our country's hammer was—as no one doubted—bigger than his, and yet what might have happened if we had used finer, subtler tools to do the same job, perhaps more slowly to be sure, but without pounding a country to save it?

Let's look at the job that was done in Iraq: On the plus side, a cruel tyrant was driven from power. On the minus side, like so many tyrants before him he was not weighed in the scales of international justice. On the plus side, our country may have determined the future of Iraq and its resources. On the minus side, we have earned the life-long enmity of Muslims world-wide. On the plus side, we have secured the rich resources of a small Eastern country for Western civilization. On the minus side, we have lost the priceless cultural heritage of the world's oldest civilization. (Parenthetically, Gandhi was reportedly asked what he thought of Western Civilization. He answered, "I think it would be a good idea.")

On the plus side in Iraq, we have freed millions from the pounding of a dictator who nevertheless shared their culture, language, history and religion. On the minus side, we have subjected the same millions to the pounding by an even greater power which shares none of this with them, which has hammered their cities, schools, markets, and hospitals, and has killed thousands of innocent women, children and the elderly.

And worst of all, we have proclaimed to the whole world the fraudulent and lethal lesson that the Bigger Hammer is the best. No wonder India, Pakistan, China, North Korea, Iran, Israel, Russia, and others are eagerly forging Bigger Nuclear Hammers to pound the world into dust, as we have taught them. Figure it out. The war in Iraq has not been won. No war is won. It is only over for a time, until the pounding starts again.

The Big Hammer will create nothing more than a pile of rubble that others more wise, skillful and loving than you will labor long and hard to rebuild, all the while cursing your heavy-handed, careless and shoddy work. The greatest country in the world can do better than this. Any carpenter knows if you force it too hard, you break it. Use the smaller hammer. Use the finer tool. Use your skill, your knowledge, your wisdom, your experience, your gentleness, your patience, your eye, your art, your heart—especially your heart—and you can create beauty that will last for ages.

Shad Bloom

Love is happening all around us these days. It's almost enough to make you blush, really. Giving off their beguiling aromas, the flowers of the shad, cherry, apple, lilac, elm and maple are shamelessly pollinating each other with the bees playing the match-maker. Wearing their bright colors, the violets, bluets, dandelions and wild strawberries are each and all frantically fertilizing their own kind. Singing their enchanting songs the birds are homemaking everywhere. We've got robins nesting in the garage, mourning doves in the pine trees and pileated woodpeckers in the old ash by the church. Along the streets in town the young hold hands, and the old hold hands on the porch swing. We breathe in love with every breath, and sometimes sneeze from the total intoxication of it.

Love is such a universal phenomenon right now that the natural philosopher cannot help but conclude that love is a quality embedded in the universe, a passionate desire for ever more love and beauty to be energetically worked out in the Creation again and again by a loving Creator.

The materialistic scientist will ever-so predictably respond by saying, "No, no, it is not so! Love is nothing but a far-fetched, soft-minded, wooly-headed myth. All of this apparent beauty and desire and passion is only the scientific principle of evolution at work, the soul-less and random replicating of complex physical and chemical structures with no more purpose or meaning than the passing on of selfish genes."

The fatal flaw in the materialistic argument is not about evolution. Evolution is nothing more or less than a way through which the love of the Creator is expressed in this world. The fatal flaw in the materialistic argument is much more fundamental, and it is simply this: To whom would you rather make love: someone who brings you soul-less, spirit-less, self-centered and dreary theories, or someone who brings you fragrant flowers, poetry, sweet songs and fine fragrances? To whom would you rather give yourself, body and soul: someone who tells you it's all meaningless and mechanical or someone who tells you it's love that makes the world go around? With whom would you rather roll around and replicate: the materialist or the lover of Nature?

The answer is easy. Nature already knows it, and so do you. Go out today into the blooming and buzzing confusion, and see for yourself. Materialists breed more and more morbid theories. Lovers breed more and more tender lovers. Evolution does the rest. Make love and be patient and steadfast like the birds and the bees, season after season. *Amor omnia vincit*. Love will conquer all. It's just a matter of time.

MEMORIAL DAY

On Memorial Day many of us around here still remember Fred Fehrle who used to head up the parade wearing his Navy uniform that still fit him when he was in his 70s. He'd borrow a bike from one of the kids and ride it facing backwards in front of the Legion Hall until it was time to march.

When I was still a green preacher, and Fred was the church sexton, I had the words to the Lord's Prayer taped to the pulpit. When he saw that piece of paper Fred laughed out loud and said, "That reminds me of the ship's captain who would give orders from the bridge. Every now and then he'd take out a piece of paper from his coat pocket and look at it; then he'd go back to giving orders."

"One day he left his coat hanging on a hook and some of the men got the mate to reach into the pocket and take out the paper. It said, 'Port, Left. Starboard, Right.'"

It's human nature to commemorate those who have died. In our town, we go to the Old Cemetery of 1794 after church on Sunday to remember those who have died in the past. As we walk among the silent stones we learn that children and young adults died much more often from disease than they do today. Women died in childbirth more often. They had an easy familiarity with death that seems strange today. On the stone of Adeline Sophia Faulkner, died March 1, 1833 aged 3 years, 8 months, 9 days we read:

"Relentless death will have its prey/ Nor youth nor health its hand can stay/Yes, little child, as you pass by/Look and be warned, you too must die."

We also find that our ancestors believed they were going on to a far more glorious life than this one. The graves in the Old Cemetery are pointed to the East so that those who sleep in them might see the first light of dawn on the Last Day, and be resurrected into Eternal Life. Here is the inscription on the gravestone of Warren Osgood, aged 31:

"How sure the fate, how sad the doom, that unto dust, dust must return/How clear the truth that saints will rise/ to join their Savior in the skies."

Furthermore, our walk in the Old Cemetery teaches us how important it was to our forbears to be prepared for death. The marker for Susanna Ellis, aged 31, reads:

"Behold, my friend, see here I lie/Think on your end, prepare to die."

On Monday, Memorial Day, we go to the parade to remember those who have died in war. The Legion Hall overflows with veterans and their wives and children. The cannon is fired and the church bell is somberly tolled. In a field across the street the local Peace & Justice group has planted a white flag for every American soldier who has died in Iraq. It's respectful and moving.

We have a fine parade with everything from loud fire engines to decorated bicycles, and of course the high school marching band. It's a rather small parade, so they turn around after prayers at the cemetery and march back. This means we get to see both sides of the parade without crossing the street. Then, there's the public picnic at the parsonage. The Memorial Day parade is a fine civic event, but it isn't really a celebration because there is a monumental burden of pain borne in it.

The pain of Memorial Day comes from the human costs of war. I have an uncle and a brother who are veterans, and many friends who served in Vietnam. They grew up in the lingering glory of World War II, which has been called "the Last Good War," and its veterans have been called "the Greatest Generation." That is part of the pain for veterans of later wars like Korea, Vietnam, the Gulf War, and Iraq. The righteousness of these wars was not so clear, nor so widely recognized by the public. That's very painful. So, the human costs of more recent wars are not only physical— loss of life and limb and loved ones. They are also psychological and spiritual—loss of innocence and righteousness.

This loss comes in part from the knowledge that over the last century the costs of war have fallen on civilians far more than on combatants by a factor of about ten to one. The death of innocents in Dresden and Hiroshima, My Lai and Fallujah, and countless other towns, cities and countries have tainted the glory of war and raised the guilt. Some younger veterans still focus on the glory, as the young will. But, even more stand silent and weep as the flags go by; or they simply stay home and try over and over again to forget.

It's time for healing. It is good to honor the combat veterans of war: they were trying their utmost to do right. But, we also need to remember the millions of innocent civilian victims of combat. And more, we have to face the hard truth that modern warfare has lost its glory simply because it has lost its righteousness. It no longer solves as much as it savages. If we are to survive as a species, then we need to grow beyond war. We have ancient and hard-earned knowledge of the pain and costs of war, and we have new and wiser ways of solving our conflicts.

On Memorial Day we can honor our brave vets and all the dead, we can weep for the incalculable suffering, and then we

can all begin together to march beyond war with the same dili-
gence and determination that we once marched into war. There
are truer and nobler ways to give our lives. That's the new path
to glory.

Julia Ward Howe was a reformer, women's suffragist, aboli-
tionist, preacher, and world peace activist. In 1861 she wrote this
about how to give our lives:

"In the beauty of the lilies Christ was born across the sea/with
a glory in his bosom that transfigures you and me/As he died to
make men holy, let us live to make men free/As God is marching
on."

Walter Rauschenbusch, the prophet of the Social Gospel,
admired more and more as years go by, wrote this prayer back
in 1910:

"O Lord, break thou the spell of the enchantments that make
the nations drunk with the lust of battle and draw them on as
willing tools of death. Grant us a quiet and steadfast mind when
our own nation clamors for vengeance or aggression. Strengthen
our sense of justice and our regard for the equal worth of other
peoples and races. Grant to the rulers of nations faith in the possibility of peace through justice... Bless our soldiers and sailors
for their swift obedience and their willingness to answer to the
call of duty, but inspire them nonetheless with a hatred for war...
May our young still rejoice to die for their country with the valor
of their fathers, but teach our age nobler methods of matching
our strength, and more effective ways of giving our lives."

Deep is the desire in human hearts to find nobler ways of giving our lives. We want to die for others, not just for ourselves.
We want to give up our lives willingly for something greater than
ourselves: for our loved ones, for our family or tribe, for our
country, our religion, but most of all for more love, for more life,
for God.

But, the war-makers, who entice others to fight while they
themselves remain safe from harm and profit from the suffering,

can and will deceive greatly. We may heed their call to heroism, to God and country and flag, to fight and die for what is right, thinking this a nobler way of giving our lives. Then, we find that we have been deceived. We find that the good done by war is far outweighed by the harm. We find that the ones who profited most were the Masters of War themselves, not the brave soldiers, and certainly not the innocent victims.

Rauschenbush concludes:

"O Lord, since first the blood of Abel cried to thee from the ground that drank it, this earth of thine has been defiled with the blood of man shed by his brother's hand and the centuries sob with the ceaseless horror of war. Ever the pride of kings and the covetousness of the strong has driven peaceful nations to slaughter. Ever the songs of the past and the pomp of armies have been used to inflame the passions of the people... Teach our age, O Lord, nobler ways of giving our lives."

GENIUS

Anyone who has lived in these parts for long will tell you that certain places have an intangible presence or "spirit" that seems to inhabit them, quite apart from their natural beauty. You can go to such places alone, yet you are not alone while you are there. In my experience, the Blue Hill Falls and the Mountain are such places. There is the trail along Patten Brook. There are the Reversing Falls at the meeting of Dennys, Whiting and Cobscook Bays. There is a little pure spring which flows out of a hillside into a pool lined with buttercups and watercress near the Little Falls of the Pennamaquan River in Washington County. Every time I go there for spring water the presence is very real, though diffuse and undefined. Places where land and water meet, mountain-tops, waterfalls, wells and springs, caves, huge boulders, and other unusual natural formations often have this spiritual presence.

The ancient Romans called this guardian spirit a "genius." They called it "the genius of the place." People, too, might possess this guardian spirit or genius. In ancient times it was seen as a gift. It was said that someone had a genius for something, or a gift for something. This was natural. When the Christian church moved into Europe, these primitive geniuses or guardian spirits of places were declared to be replaced by the spirit of some long-dead human 'saint,' thus giving the Church a sort of ownership over the power places, since the Church decided who was a saint and who was not; and assigned particular saints to particular places. This is un-natural. It is spiritual colonialism.

In more modern or post-modern times we have again changed the way we talk about genius. Now we say that a person is gifted, or is a genius. This suggests that the person owns or possesses the spirit, when in truth the spirit possesses the person. Now, a person who has been given a genius somehow sees it as their own. It makes them, not simply more fortunate, but somehow better—as though they had gifted themselves, or made themselves into a genius. Today, we say that Albert Einstein was a genius; though he apparently was not a genius at organizing his study, or at being a husband or parent, or at handling money. It might be more truthful to say that he had a genius or a gift for mathematics.

Every place is given a genius of some kind. Every creature is given a genius for something. If the waterfall fills us with its extraordinary spirit; if the brown thrasher sings with a gift for subtle mimicry and improvisation far beyond other birds; if Einstein discovers the theory of relativity with a genius for physics and mathematics far beyond other mortals, then how can we praise the place or the bird or the man without praising even more the Spirit which gives all gifts and every sort of genius?

THE OLD REGULATOR

The moon regulates the tides. The movement of the earth regulates the seasons determining when creatures will mate, give birth and let their young go free, and when the plants will bloom and go to seed to provide food for all the animals. And so it has been since time immemorial. We can go against these regular rhythms if we wish, but to do so is costly and even disastrous. That is because we are all part of a great self-regulating system that has evolved to provide enough, but not too much, for everyone. It's called Nature. Nature regulates all things so that all life can continue to thrive and survive.

The government regulates who can drive and how fast, who can marry and at what age, who can wire your house and what the codes will be, who can practice medicine, who can clean your teeth, who can give you a tattoo. The government regulates public drinking water, land-fills, how many fish you can catch and when. The government even regulates what time it is and a thousand other things for the expressed purpose of preventing harm to the majority of citizens. Then why in the world doesn't the government regulate how much interest can be charged on a loan, or how much profit can be taken from the pockets of the people? Exxon Mobil showed a profit of $11 billion for its shareholders in the first quarter of 2008. That could be buying tons of rice and beans, but instead it's buying pounds of steak and caviar.

We are seeing a perfect storm of high prices, high unemployment, and volatile markets that is destroying people worldwide. The Free Marketeers glibly declare that only the semi-divine "Invisible Hand" should regulate the market and if some suffer or starve, don't fret, the market will eventually adjust: it's just natural selection. So, is the world soon to be populated only by oil execs and investment bankers at their shiny desks? Who will grow their food or catch their lobsters? Who will drive them to work? Who will clean their gleaming buildings? Who will fix their sewers, elevators and air conditioning? Who will tend their lawns and pools?

Today, while the poor struggle and the middle class slides toward poverty, the politicians and pundits prattle over petty talking-points like a Punch and Judy puppet show loudly acting out imaginary battles, while real live people slowly starve and freeze thinking there is something wrong with themselves. I met a good woman not long ago whose household included 7 adults and 6 children, down from 10 adults and 9 children because she had to throw some relatives out. They were low on food, had a disconnect notice on their electricity, and had missed a mortgage payment. Will they all be living somewhere under a bridge next year?

This is the real story today, so listen: There is indeed an Invisible Hand, but it's not the hand of Adam Smith or Ben Bernanke. It is the hand of Nature's God and it is going to smack the greedy mighty hard. But it will be too late for too many unless the Congress and candidates wake up to what is really going down in this country we have loved. Government is not regulating big money because big money is regulating government. The unfettered greed of the few is a metastasizing cancer threatening the lives of the many. It must be cut out quickly if the great American experiment is to survive.

FLAG DAY

Flag Day was not always a big day in town, but that changed soon after the bombing of Baghdad in March of '03. Right across from the American Legion Hall on Main Street, the local Peace and Justice group set up a memorial to soldiers and civilians who were dying in the Iraq war. They placed tiny white flags in the field for every soldier that died and a sign with a running count of American and Iraqi deaths.

Some of the Legion men were unhappy that the Iraqi dead were being counted, but others said, "As long as it's done with respect, it's OK." Then, the Legion began putting the stars and stripes on every utility pole for a mile along Main Street. I talk with both groups and have asked them both to cross the street and talk with each other. So far as I know, that hasn't happened yet. I feel bad about that. When people of the same town, race, language, and religion can't cross that street to talk, it makes you wonder how we're ever going to have peace in the world. There's still time, though.

Dear Thomas,

Thank you for your invitation to take part in the up-coming flag dedication at the Legion Hall. I was proudly elected flag-saluter in 4th grade and received the American Legion award in 8th grade. I went to the Boy Scout jamboree at Valley Forge in '57. I was a Patriot's Day re-enactor for years in Concord, Massachusetts. Being an asthmatic seminary student, I was not drafted during the Vietnam War. In fact, I actively opposed it. I think our country and our flag are beautiful. I wear a flag pin in my lapel on Sunday. After 9/11 I set up an American flag inside our church.

But, being a preacher and an Independent with a wide Libertarian streak, I do not always support the actions of our government. I think that the flag should not be forced on anyone. Seen too much, the flag is in danger of being exploited and trivialized. The best place for the flag is on a flagpole like the one at the Legion Hall where it can be tended daily and lowered at night and during inclement weather. To fly it on every utility pole in town is a bit like having a street preacher every hundred feet. You get tired of their message pretty fast, and eventually ignore it altogether. I don't think that is your intention.

Our love and respect for our country cannot be measured by the number of Chinese-made American flags we fly on public utility poles to be soaked by rain, tattered by wind, scorched by sun, and spattered and torn by passing trucks. Our love and respect for our country can be measured best by our love and respect for each other. That's my opinion.

Having said that, I will do my best at the flag dedication on June 14. I just want you to know how I feel.

Yours sincerely,

Rob McCall

We might ask, "Is the American flag a war flag, or a peace flag." If the red stands only for the blood of American soldiers, and not for the blood of innocent civilians who died in our wars, then it is a war flag. If the blue stands only for the sky over our country and not the same sky over every other land, then it is a war flag. If the white stands only for white skin or white lies, and not white bandages to bind up the world's wounds, then it is a war flag. If the stars stand only for the fifty United States, and not for the stars in the eyes of all the world's children or the heavenly stars which shine down on all nations alike, then it is a war flag.

But if the red stands for the living blood pulsing in the veins of every earthly human instead of the spilled blood of the wounded and dying, then it is a peace flag. If the blue stands for pure air for all to breathe and pure water for all to drink and not just the blue of gun-metal, then it is a peace flag. If the white stands for the peaceable kingdom that prophets and politicians preach and not for a blinding, burning nuclear flash, then it is a peace flag. If the stars stand for the morning stars singing together on the day we stop attacking each other all the while screaming "Peace! Peace!", then it is a peace flag.

The flag stands for what we stand for. What will it be then: a war flag or a peace flag?

Summer

Sun Worship

It is easy to see why sun-worship is still the world's oldest religion. When the sun rises to its highest point in the sky and shines fully on us, we are truly re-created, we become new beings. The deep-down cold is driven from our bones by the summer sun and we feel at home once again in a friendly world, as far removed from the cold, gray, grudging sun of mid-winter as Heaven is removed from Hell. No matter how hard we may try to remember the rich luxuries of summer during the cold of winter, no fading memory can come close to the actual living again of these fulsome days.

Now, even the daisies turn their bright faces to follow the sun as it moves across the sky, so devout is their worship and profound their affection for the Source of all Life and all Light. Small creatures like the numerous kinds of bees begin their lively motions at dawn and keep busy until dusk when they retire again, plump-full and satisfied with their day's work upon the glowing flowers from which they derive food, drink, medicine, materials for building, and all things needful for their simple and true, harmless and honest lives. See how every possible shape, color and fragrance of the cosmos is embodied in the flowers, leaves and branches of plants. See how every possible motion, motive, sense and sound from the whole realm of Nature is so elegantly expressed by the insects, birds and wild creatures.

We walk in a wholly other world these days, a world of mercy and healing. A holy host of blooming, buzzing, beaming beings blesses us with the kind ministrations of their actual, mortal love for life. We are redeemed to the depths of our ragged souls. We come all apart. We are knitted back together. We are made whole again. Gosh, it's great.

Now, where did I put the bug-dope?

AT CAMP

Thirty years ago when we built our camp on Cobscook Bay in Washington County, the easternmost in Maine, it seemed like wilderness, and really it was. People got lost in the woods there in those days. We made a small clearing and framed the cabin with the trees we cut down. The woods were close on every side, but over time we gradually cleared them away, and the woods seemed less wild. One day, not a hundred feet from our cabin, we discovered a huge boulder left by the glacier, settled comfortably into the ground, draped with brilliant green moss on its North side, its top littered with the fallen needles of spruce and fir. For a long time, we had not even known it was there. Its discovery was a revelation: A mighty rock within a weary land. Our delight was great with this touchstone, this anchor on the changing land. It was older than anything else we saw under the sky. Now we watch it from the cabin. We go out to sit upon it and feel its comforting inertia, its patience, its peace. We called it "Tunkashila" which is a Lakota word meaning "grandfather rock" or simply "God."

Sometimes I imagine all the changes this grandfather rock has seen since the glaciers left it sitting there 12,000 years ago on cold, bare bedrock scraped clean by the ice. Back then, the little brook next to the boulder ran with milky ice-melt, and the winds from the north blew bitter cold over the retreating glaciers. After a time, I imagine, lichens and mosses took hold on the surrounding bedrock, their decaying bodies building a thin topsoil to support the seeds of spruce, fir and birch dropped by squirrels and jays as they slowly spread the forests northward from subglacial climes in what is now Massachusetts.

For thousands of years the first Americans hunted in the woods and fished and clammed along the shores of Cobscook Bay, maybe camping by our boulder, using it as a landmark, a sitting place and a windbreak for their fires, while spruce and fir sprouted, grew great, and fell to enrich the soil for their offspring. All the while, our boulder sat motionless as thousands of generations of mosses flourished and died upon it, thousands of generations of red squirrels shucked fir cones on it, and thousands of generations of ravens croaked and strutted and picked at the leavings, while the eagles soared above and the loons and seals called from the bay.

When the whites came—in this case the Irish some 240 years ago—they cleared the forests and ranged sheep, goats and cattle over the land. I imagine a big Galloway bull scraping off his winter coat, or a goat scampering up on our boulder bathed in sun. After World War I, the farm was abandoned, and the fields grew up to woods again, wrapping our silent, abiding boulder in the cool dark of the forest for another 75 years, until the day we began cutting trees for our cabin and the sun shone upon it again, as it does today. "Change and decay in everything I see," sings the old hymn, "O Thou who changes not, abide with me."

At our camp, as we like to say, "the power never goes out." That is because there is no electricity; also no phone or running water, and no road to the cabin door. Everything is carried in, or there already. The power, however, is plentifully provided by the meeting of earth, air, fire and water and by the enveloping silence.

Water does its work as fog and showers kept everything damp, but we managed to get a good lot of our work done. Fire did its work too as the woodstove dried our soggy things and the kerosene lights illuminated our reading at night. The profound silence sets your ears whispering for a day or so until it sinks in. You can hear the mandibles of a bald-faced hornet gathering wood fibers from the shingles. You can almost hear the slugs singing.

For about 25 years I mowed a couple of acres by hand with scythe and grass-whip. When I turned 60, I ruefully but gratefully accepted the gift of a roaring old power mower with big wheels that does the job in a third of the time. I try to hit the rocks at just the right angle so instead of dulling the blade, they sharpen it. It occurred to me that the American obsession with mowing is a way of clinging to the last vestiges of agriculture in an urbanized society. Just the way a sheep dog will herd chickens or cats or children if it has no sheep to herd, we zealously mow the grass as though we were making food for someone, even though we're making nothing but noise and smoke.

Rebecca is highly skilled at providing food and comfort under primitive camp conditions and we have a blissful time. For amusement, I play the apple box fiddle I made back in my orchard days. One damp morning I was playing *Sheebag Sheemore* to the fog, but somehow it just didn't sound right. I shook the fiddle and heard a rattling inside. Opening it up, I shook out a huge mouse nest of shredded leaves, feathers, pillow stuffing and bits of black ribbon. This improved the sound of the fiddle, but only slightly. I also found a yellow jacket nest in the ground in the very place where many summers ago I was stung for scything carelessly over it, suggesting that yellow jackets return to their favorite places, too. Chipmunks were more numerous than red squirrels this year for the first time in memory. Chippies make much better company: they are friendly and curious and don't act as though they own the place as the red squirrels do.

Several times I paddled out in the fog to go seal hunting on the

Bay. The trophy I sought was not pelt or meat, but a meeting with the harbor seals that loll on the ledges. I was not disappointed. One burly male scout with whiskers dripping followed me around and slapped the water to see if I would retreat. I stayed, enjoying the ethereal sensation of rising and falling in the foggy void out of sight of shore.

In the fields the ox-eye daisies, orange and yellow hawkweed, yellow rattle, purple vetch and blue-eyed grass offer all the colors of the rainbow to our wondering eyes. In the ditches and swamps the wild iris or 'Blue Flag' flaunts its Buddhist blooms to sooth the fevered mind with mystic beauty. In the woods the new growth on spruce, fir and tamarack is soft and pale green, dripping jewels in the fog.

In this land by the sea where the chipmunk stores seeds in a bird's nest, the bears fertilize the blueberries, and the loons and the mourning doves call to each other, is it the stern law of tooth and claw, bloodshed and competition we see all around? Is it all struggle and the survival of the fittest? It is if we are seeing with only one eye. But if we are seeing with both eyes, it is the sweet law of nesting and seeding and feeding and mutuality. It is the survival of the kindest.

While joyfully engaged in the Sisyphean task of cutting brush on the high bank along the shore I was treated to one of the most elemental natural events when the sound of thunder and the sight of strange, tortured clouds in the North gave me pause. An unfamiliar roar coming across the waters of the bay sent me scurrying up to the cabin just seconds before the heavens opened with the most horrendous hail-storm I've ever seen. Bushels of nickel- to quarter-sized hail-stones hammered upon the roof and bounced in the grass like thousands of pale, manic grasshoppers while thunder and lightning tore the sky. Fresh green leaves torn from the trees fluttered down all around as I stood awe-struck and heart pounding by the open window. At the height of the tumult, the cool sound of a lone robin's rain-song floated through the woods.

A torrential rain followed the hail, until the storm passed to the South. I ventured out to gather from white patches on the ground a handful of hail-stones with a pure white pea-sized center surrounded by more or less crystal clear ice. I ate a few to taste the pure sweetness of this sublime water, drawn from the sea by the heat of the sun, lifted in clouds to the cold high atmosphere until they grew too heavy for the sky to hold them, then fell of their own weight down to our great delight. What an honor, what an elemental sacrament, to taste this bread and wine of the high heavens down here on earth.

INDEPENDENCE DAY

There are few things we value more than our independence. When asked what they believe, most Congregationalists will immediately get a little flushed and say in a rather loud voice something to the effect that "each congregation is independent and no larger body can tell us who our minister will be, how we will do business, or what we will believe!"

Our small towns are much the same way. For years I have been doing an informal traffic survey from my study window at the parsonage. If there is no traffic coming on Main Street, roughly 80% of Maine cars *ignore* the STOP sign at the end of Parker Point Road. This seems to include everything from BMW's to large SUVs. At the same time, out-of-state cars currently run the stop sign less often, about 40%. My conclusions? Small town Mainers are plain independent.

Radicalism of both the left and the right flourishes on American soil. Both liberals and conservatives grumble about the government. We cheat on our taxes. Land-owners insist, "It's my land and I can do whatever I want with it." "Not in my backyard" becomes the mantra of the nation. A few years back one Texas extremist declared the land around his trailer to be the 'Independent Republic of Texas' and was ready to shoot at people who did not recognize his independence.

Believe me, I appreciate my independence, too, and can get ugly if deprived of it. But it's possible to get too extreme about it. The ultimate independence would be to do whatever we want to, whenever we want to, without regard to the effect on others. That might be all right for a four-year-old, because we expect him to outgrow it. But in a nation of adults the result can be what the sociologists call *anomie*, the collapse of society into atomistic particles that no longer bond, and what the psychologists call *sociopathic behavior*, no shared 'core values,' only those of each individual.

In *The Weekly Packet*, our local paper, Michael Berliner of the Ayn Rand Institute wrote: "To the Founding Fathers there was no authority higher than the individual mind, not King George, not God, not society."

On Independence Day we might reasonably ask whether the *Declaration of Independence* supports this view. We may be surprised at what we find in this seminal statement of human rights in American history.

First, we find only one statement about the independent rights of the individual: *We hold these truths to be self-evident, that all Men are created equal...* But even this statement continues by declaring our dependence on God for those rights: *...that they are endowed by their Creator with certain inalienable rights...*

In times like these, we must declare again in the strongest possible terms that the rights of life, liberty and the pursuit of happiness enumerated in the *Declaration* derive not from any nation or government, not from any church or court or Congress, not from any army, nor from any earthly person or power. These rights are endowed equally to all people by the Creator. They are God-given, and no human can take them away from another without incurring the righteous judgment of Heaven.

75

The next statement declares our *dependence* on government—that is, our neighbors and each other—for the preservation of those rights: *That to secure these rights, governments are instituted... deriving their just Powers from the Consent of the Governed...*

The next statement reiterates our interdependence on each other: *...that whenever any Form of Government becomes destructive of these Ends, it is the Right of the People to alter or abolish it...* Let me repeat that. *Whenever any Form of Government becomes destructive of these Ends, it is the Right of the People to alter or abolish it.*

We find statement after statement about our interdependence with God and each other, yet nowhere do we find any statement on the independence of the individual. The word "individual" does not even appear in the *Declaration of Independence.*

Further evidence that this was a declaration of interdependence is put forth by Pauline Maier in *American Scripture, Making the Declaration of Independence.* Traditionally, the document has been viewed as the independent inspiration of one individual—Thomas Jefferson. Maier's research reveals that between April and early July of 1776 at least 90 declarations of independence from Britain were drafted by Massachusetts towns, New York guilds and militias, New York, Maryland and Virginia counties, South Carolina grand juries, and the legislatures of nine of the 13 colonies. The Continental Congress was not unaware of these other declarations, and several were drawn upon in drafting the final version of July 4, 1776. Cleary, even the drafting of the *Declaration of Independence,* was an interdependent effort.

It is my opinion that the strong themes of interdependence with God and each other expressed in this formative document draw heavily on Christian traditions. Few, if any, of the authors, editors, and legislators who enacted it were unfamiliar with the New Testament; and the emphasis on God and neighbor in the final draft is very clear.

Jesus declares our interdependence in the Sermon on the Mount:

"Love God, love your neighbor... (and) love your enemy, so that you may be children of God... (who) makes the sun rise on the evil and the good (alike) and the rain fall on the just and unjust."

Paul declares our interdependence in the first letter to the Corinthians: "The body does not consist of one member, but of many... If one member suffers, all suffer together; if one member is honored, all rejoice together."

Common sense agrees. If we are really independent of each other, then the poisons we pour into our rivers will not go downstream to poison others. The toxins we put into the air will not blow into the next state to suffocate others. Our disdain and neglect of the poor and their children will have no effect upon them or upon us. Our hatred and suspicion of those who are different in race, or religion, or politics, or ideology will have no effect upon them or upon us. The violence we visit on other nations will not return to us, and we will not reap what we sow.

If, however, we are interdependent, as Jesus and Paul and the founders of our country believed, and common sense proves, then the consequences of hatred or disdain or neglect will most surely fall upon us all alike; rich and poor, old and young. If we are interdependent, our behavior will have consequences, not just for ourselves, but for the whole body; whether the town, the nation, the world, or the Creation. So it follows that our evil or thoughtless acts hurt all others regardless of their guilt or innocence, just as the rain falls on the just and the unjust. Likewise, our good works benefit all others regardless of their evil or their goodness, just as the sun shines on the evil and the good. We do reap what we sow.

Like it or not, we are profoundly interdependent upon each other for our welfare. Benjamin Franklin said it memorably at the signing of the *Declaration*: "Gentlemen, we must all hang together, or most assuredly, we shall all hang separately."

The closing words of the *Declaration* of July 4, 1776 will serve as the conclusion to this essay. They display a degree of courage,

unselfishness, and maturity in actual human politicians that
might make one yearn for those times, or yearn for that stature
of leadership in these times. But we need not wait for our leaders.
If we lead, they will follow.

May the spirit of '76 be renewed in each of us today, not just
for ourselves or our nation, but for all people, all nations, and all
creatures. May the last words of that document be our declaration of interdependence:

> *"With a firm reliance on the Protection of divine Providence,
> we mutually pledge to each other our Lives, our Fortunes,
> and our sacred Honor."*

LUNA MOTHS

On a warm July day I went over the blueberry barrens lined with black-eyed Susan, brook lobelia and even a startling orange wood lily, down to Billings Pond, also called First Pond, a very shallow, narrow, reedy pond of perhaps a mile in length and a quarter mile or less at its widest. A beaver dam presently determines its depth. It is the home of beavers, otters, ducks, herons, loons, frogs, turtles and the legendary whistling snake, as well as other living mysteries. Patches of white and yellow pond lilies, blue arrowhead, rushes and sedges stretch between shores lined with yellow swamp lousewort so that the paddler cannot proceed in a straight line but must navigate around them.

On this day there was a light, foggy breeze off the bay from the South and dark clouds threatening thunder showers rolled overhead from the Northwest. Waterstriders sketched nervous V's over the surface, bullfrogs plucked their bass notes, and a loon floated majestically as a royal barge in the breeze. I paddled upstream about half the length of the pond to a small island which is centered in the widest, wildest place. I got out to sit on the rocks and soak my feet in the tea-colored water while eating a tin of kippered herring. The pond was quiet, but not silent. The sounds of wind, bird and frog were so faint that the effect was of an active hush, very remote and primitive. In all directions, things were just as they had been since the glaciers retreated and ice-melt-water roared through this long, deep cleft in the rocks.

The sky began to get darker as I finished eating and I paddled out in a wide swing to the Northeast of the island before heading back downstream to the place I put in. As my eye glanced over the water, a faint green in the reeds ahead, much paler than the arrowhead leaves, caught and fixed my gaze. Whatever it was, its color was vegetable, but its form was animal; a symmetrical blunt triangle with a tail. As I floated closer I recognized the light green translucence of a perfect Luna moth perched on a single, shivering reed, the trailing tips of its wings just inches above the water. I held my breath. The cool moth was like a Japanese paper cutting, poised above its up-ended reflection. As I glided by, I could see the furry white body, feathery buff antennae and eye-spots on the broad wings held perpendicular like a kite to the wind. This shy, rare nocturnal moth rested in plain sight in the midday light.

Here I was, floating almost close enough to touch one of the most reticent and secret spirits of the summer. And as if that weren't enough, my eye caught another larger Luna on another thin reed a few feet away in precisely the same posture and orientation. The second seemed even brighter green than the first, and was equally still as I paddled back and forth around and around them, feasting my eyes on their haunting beauty and utter passivity—the holy angels of Billings Pond.

Here is what the moths said silently to me: "Turn away from the false Shroud of Turin. Forget your Lost Ark of the Covenant. Pay no mind to the fragments of the True Cross, the Weeping Icons of Mary, the face of Christ in the wall-paper, the Chariots of Fire, the Tooth of the Buddha, your Stonehenge TV specials. Turn instead toward the living angels, the Luna moths, the flowers of the field, the birds of the air, authentic breathing miracles right before your eyes. Turn to them. Turn and be saved.

CROWS

The *New York Times* and many others reported experiments at the University of Washington that "have found that crows and their relatives (blue jays, ravens, magpies) can recognize individual human faces and act accordingly." These members of the Corvid family are known throughout history and myth for their sharp intelligence and keen interest in human affairs. In the Noah legend, the first bird sent from the ark was a Corvid, and through the ages ravens were carried aboard ships because of their ability to fly directly toward the nearest land. Corvids fed Elijah hiding out in the wilds from death at the hands of the ruthless king he had challenged. In Aesop's fable, the crow figures out how to get a drink by dropping rocks in a jug to raise the water level. For the Northwest tribes, Raven is the Trickster and Creator of the World, even riding along on the primordial flood with other animals as in the Noah legend. Other scientific peer-reviewed experiments have shown that Corvids can count, use tools, mimic other sounds, and speak and even understand human language. Blue jays can remember hundreds of sites where they have hidden acorns.

Given their widely-known and well-documented intelligence, it's not so surprising that Corvids can recognize and discriminate between human faces. What is *really* surprising is that given humans' widely-known and well-documented intelligence, most of us can't tell one crow from another. We really need to get out more.

GOLDFINCHES

We've been greatly delighted by the goldfinches flitting and tumbling through the late summer air like flying yellow flowers with their delicate chirping, sipping at the bird bath, and generally showing a preternatural joy in their motions and music to the point where one wonders how anything so small can survive—never mind flourish—in such a rough and raw world. The sparkling, magical presence of goldfinches has mitigated some of the sadder events.

We had to put down our good old black dog Quoddy just short of his 14th birthday. In sharing the news with friends and neighbors we came to realize that nearly everyone has endured a similar ending at some time in their lives. Our grief at these times is so pure because dogs are so pure an expression of life: forgiving, loyal, always up for any adventure; without complicated psychological dynamics or mind games. They never try to be what they are not and are unfailingly authentic and true to their own nature and heritage, however mixed. No matter how much we train them to our human ways, the true dog always comes through: stealing cheese, chewing shoes, sleeping on the

couch, barking at shadows. We're ever grateful to the good veter-
inarian who came to our house to administer the stroke of grace:
a hard job—especially with three of us standing around bawling
our eyes out. We're also surprised and grateful for the cards and
other true expressions of sympathy.

Also sad was the recent loss of several elm trees in the village to the elm disease. One was among the biggest left in town.
My heart goes out to the hardy tree men who dearly love trees
and must, like the vet who loves animals, administer the final
stroke of grace to such a magnificent, dying creature and bear
it to the ground. One good thing is that we can now see the
golden weather-vane on the church steeple while we're making
our morning coffee in the parsonage kitchen and so predict the
day's weather. It's a small comfort.

Saddest of all is the daily news of elders who cannot buy their
medicines, middle-aged workers who have lost their jobs and
pensions, and children world-wide on their way to school who
must avoid predatory men, suicide-killers, and bombs falling
from the sky.

I hope they all have something like goldfinches tumbling and
highly chanting through the air to brighten their days. I hope they
have something like goldfinches to show them that small, delicate, beautiful, hopeful, musical life will survive in the face of the
lifeless, heartless, hungry mechanisms which we still relentlessly
manufacture to devour the elements, and to which we still seem
willing to sacrifice all that is sweet and soulful.

GRASSHOPPERS

"It is he that sitteth upon the circle of the earth, and the inhabitants thereof are as grasshoppers...(It is he) that stretcheth out the heavens..., that bringeth the princes to nothing." — Isaiah 40:22-23

It may not be the Day of the Locust yet, but it certainly is the day of its cousin, the grasshopper. A walk through the grass these days may loose a torrent of grasshoppers jumping merrily in every direction. (Your commentator knows that he commits a cardinal sin among scientists by ascribing human feelings like "merriment" to a jumping grasshopper. Yet, how could it be anything but merry in using those grand hind legs for their Divine and Darwinian purpose?) Most common hereabouts are the band-winged grasshopper: order *Orthoptera*, family *Acrididae*, sub-family *Oedipodinae*. They have a hard grass-colored forewing, and a broad, bright-banded hind wing that makes them look like a butterfly when they take flight, but with a noticeable crackling sound; the song of late summer fields.

Grasshoppers hatch in the spring from eggs laid in the ground the previous fall. Jonathan Fisher, amateur naturalist in Blue Hill

170 years ago wrote, "When the Grasshopper first appears in the Spring, which is sometimes earlier, and sometimes later, according to the state of the weather (spring weather obviously hasn't changed much in 170 years (ed.), it is about the size of a common flea, and of a whitish color."

Unlike some other insects, the grasshopper has no larval stage, but looks like a tiny adult—though without wings—all through its development, during which it sheds its shell several times. Fisher continues, "When caught, it quickly besmears the fingers with a substance resembling molasses." When we were kids, we called it "tobacco juice." The grasshopper has, quite frankly, a smeared reputation. Like the locust, some years the grasshoppers emerge in huge numbers to devastate grain crops and other vegetables, causing famine. Your commentator seems to remember a monument to the seagulls that swooped in to save Mormon crops by gobbling hordes of 'hoppers in early Utah.

Then, there is Aesop's ancient fable about Grasshopper who merrily played the fiddle while Ant grimly stored up food for the coming winter. When winter came, Grasshopper begged for food from Ant only to be refused and self-righteously condemned for his merriment and lack of industry. This sounds like the classic liberal/conservative conflict.

The natural truth is quite different. The grasshopper amply provides for the next generation by laying fertile eggs in the earth, then fearlessly fiddling away its final hours until it gently gives up its life to the winter. The ant, too, is fully devoted, not to saving its own thorax, but to the care and feeding of the next generation.

When we are troubled by the bitterness of the current political debate wherein one paltry party tries to secure its own fortunes tomorrow, by tearing apart the other party today; then it's good to remember that all nations are like grasshoppers and ants in the eyes of the Creator. Like them we will soon be gone. It's also good to remember that our coming generations, like theirs, will eat the food and drink the cup we have prepared for them.

NATURAL HEALING

One of the marvels of the present growing season is seen in the power of living things to heal. Trees sometimes lose a section of bark, scraped off by a piece of machinery or the falling of another tree against them, or where a branch is pruned off. During the growing season the careful observer will notice that under and around the edges of the wound, the living bark ever-so-slowly begins to expand latitudinally over the bare dead surface to conform to it, cover it and heal the wound. The "callous," as it is called, which grows over the injury has the appearance of the bark of a young tree, even though the tree itself may be very old. The cambium layer of the bark is a plastic, flowing medium, the living plant flesh; forever young; forever trying to incorporate the wounded or broken places back into the whole body of the tree; forever trying to heal.

A similar phenomenon can be found on the surface of the ground. Perhaps a snow-plow last winter scraped the soil off an area leaving it bare and lifeless; or perhaps a larger area has been bulldozed for some narrow purpose. During the growing season this ground is gradually and naturally reseeded from living plants all around, and brought back to life. A plowed place, if left alone long enough, will repeat the primal history of the land around it by first going to grasses, brambles and weeds, then to poplars and birches; until it finally becomes a part of the surrounding forest. The natural landscape tries to incorporate any anomaly, any disturbance or wound, back into itself.

The animal body heals in a similar way. A cut or scrape or wound on the flesh is slowly closed up and restored by the healing powers of life until it is made a part of the whole body again.

Why is this so? Why is there a power to heal? It could just as well have been the case that living things were given no power to heal and would continue to be barked and plowed and wounded over and over again and eventually helplessly succumb to the accumulation of injuries that come with life in a dynamic environment. But, this is simply not the case. There is, in living things, an almost limitless power to heal.

The Spirit of life inhabits one great coherent body which brought all life into being out of a fiercely intense desire for it to be. We are not brought forth into a purely dog-eat-dog, law-of-tooth-and-claw, cold and cruel kind of place. We are not left alone and helpless against the slings and arrows of outrageous fortune, or the injuries of fate, or the wheels of destiny. We are given the gift of life which includes, yes, the possibility of hurt or injury; but also the marvelous power of healing, the power to re-incorporate every hurt, every wound, every injury—even death—back into the whole body which is life.

This power of healing is not necessary for life. The living world could surely exist without it. This power of healing is given because the world is a place of compassion not just compulsion, of love not just logistics—a place of feeling not just physics. We only need to see this power at work to make it work. We only need to get with it to get it.

GOD AND NATURE

An English clergyman of the late 18th century by the name of William Paley, and the invention of the mainspring, may be largely responsible for the idea of God shared by many of us today. If you believe in an orderly universe set in motion by an intelligent creator who exists outside of the universe, yet who designed it to function according to discernable and predictable laws which do not change; if you believe in a God who formed the universe out of soul-less matter and then backed off; if you believe in a God who intervenes only now and then in the functioning of the universe once it has been set in motion, then your God is very much like William Paley's "watch-maker" God, popularized in his book *Natural Theology; or, Evidences of the Existence and Attributes of the Deity* published in 1802. (We know, incidentally, that Jonathan Fisher read Paley, because Fisher's journals repeatedly mention him.)

William Paley's argument is this: When we find a pocket-watch lying in the field, we know someone must have manufactured it. Likewise, when we see a universe so carefully designed, we must infer the existence of a Divine Designer somewhere, even though we cannot observe one.

For two thousand years, classical theology has seen Nature as distinct and separate from God; as God's handiwork or God's servant or God's creation, as though all that our eyes can see is a manufactured product. The result is an insoluble problem which has plagued Western thought from Augustine to Einstein; the separation and alienation between spirit and flesh, mind and body, energy and matter. This separation has driven God out of Nature. The resulting alienation has led to the profaning and exploitation of Nature as a product or commodity. This now threatens the life of the Holy Body and all bodies.

Seeing Nature as different from God and from us has also led to alienation from our own bodies as parts of the Whole—being born, living, dying, and being reborn, as was Christ and as is the whole Creation. We experience disunion with God and disunion with Nature in a very similar way—fear, confusion, loss of values, anger, violence and loneliness. These maladies of modern civilization are an outgrowth of the idea of the watchmaker God who stands above and apart from the Creation—like a dim and distant Father.

Now look at the conclusions of modern post-Newtonian physics. In the past 100 years, in both the physics of the cosmos and the physics of the smallest sub-atomic particles, some startling developments have challenged the idea of the watch-maker God. Modern physics finds that different laws apply in different conditions. The laws that seem to govern planets and stars do not work with sub-atomic particles. What is more, there are vast areas of the cosmos where physicists can discern not order, but only chaos. There is random, unpredictable behavior in bodies great and small. We see light behaving as both a wave and a particle.

We are beginning to see that our laws of physics seem to be metaphors, more like poetry than calculus. Or, if you will, we are seeing that the behavior of the universe is less and less like a machine and more and more like a living being.

For too long, science and faith have been at war. The concerted effort by some to counter the teaching of evolution in the schools with questionable "creation science" is widespread. A recent Gallup poll indicated that 47% of Americans believe that God made man—as man is now—in a single act of creation within the last 10,000 years. School boards widely support the teaching of creationism along with evolution. How can we let the tenets of belief force us into such unreason? Why must we abandon reason to defend beliefs? If God gave us both the power of reason and the power of faith, shouldn't we use them both?

I would suggest that much of the anger so fiercely directed at the teaching of evolution, is not simply about a scientific theory, but about the frightening absence of the sacred and spiritual from our modern world-view. Poet Annie Dillard—a Christian but certainly not a Creationist—writes, "We have drained the light from the sacred grove. We have gone from pan-theism to pan-atheism." As Herbert Benson says, we are "hard-wired for faith." Faith in a higher power has evolved in humans just as surely as language, science, and the opposable thumb, and for good reason. Faith is just as necessary for a fulfilling life.

When we stand on top of Blue Hill mountain and scan the horizon; when we go to Schoodic Point after a storm and feel the incredible power of the ocean; when we look at the Northern lights painting the dark velvet sky, we feel welling up within us the sense of wonder at the glory and majesty of the Creation. We know that feeling to be absolutely real. Yet, when we read a science text explaining geology, meteorology, or physics, we may feel no awe, no mystery, no reverence. We look in vain to science to feed this sense of wonder that was once fed by the poetic and mythic holy stories of every culture.

"Wonder is the basis of worship," wrote Thomas Carlyle. "Science begins and ends in wonder" wrote Carl Bronowski. When we seek the atom—that thing that is irreducible—we encounter still smaller and smaller things until we reach the

Mystery. When we seek the boundaries of the universe, they expand farther and farther outward into Mystery. Whether we look inward or outward our looking ends in wonder. Every puzzle about the universe that we solve reveals an even larger puzzle of which the first solution is but a tiny piece.

To enhance our sense of wonder, here's a brief review of some astronomical research: Satellite photographs suggest that tens of thousands of icy comets containing tons of frozen water have been raining down upon the earth for billions of years. As they pass through space these comets are sheathed in carbon, the basic building block of earthly life. To quote *Time* magazine, "Suddenly it seems entirely possible that the source of much of the water on Earth—and even of life itself" might be this "gentle cosmic rain." I am not in any position to judge the validity of this research, but I am transported by the wonder of the thought—seeds of life falling from the sky. I think of Mark's gospel saying, "The kingdom of God is like scattering seeds upon the ground..."

Here is a humble suggestion: As you experience the joy, beauty and wonder of the Creation in these sweet Summer days, imagine that the mountains you see, the earth you walk upon, the water you move upon, and the sky that arches over you are not the manufactured construction of some distant mechanical engineer. Imagine instead that all you see is One Great Self-creating Body of which you are a part, to which you have belonged from the Beginning, and to which you will belong forever—the whole Creation a Great Living Creature in which you are now and will always be at home; a body that suffers, that sings and that loves you. Imagine that you are a part of the Body of God who lives, loves, suffers and dies, and ever laboriously struggles toward healing and wholeness. And wants you—one part of this Great Being which no one can comprehend, but everyone can touch and see—to be whole and healed.

I humbly suggest that you try this little experiment: Give up the idea that God is some cold, uninvolved, distant manufacturer.

Utterly discard the thought that the Earth or Nature or you or I or any creature is somehow dirty or cursed or defective or inferior. Get rid of the idea that the universe is a machine and we are only a small insignificant screw or gear in that clockwork mechanism.

Just try it. If, after a few days or weeks or months of trying, you find that casting off the old idea of a mechanistic cosmos does not inspire and heal and make you feel more welcome and at home in Creation, then go back to the old watchmaker God. That's fine. At least you'll know what time it is.

But if you are inspired and healed, then start believing that the healing and peace that we so passionately crave for ourselves and for other creatures is exactly what the Great Creation Body craves. Start imagining that the justice and righteousness that we desire for the weak and the meek and the children is just what the Creator desires. Then, at long last, come home, and be ever at home in the Great Loving Body of God.

LABOR DAY

When American workers sit down with a glass of beer or wine to celebrate the Labor Day holiday, they might be surprised to know that they hold in their hands an ancient symbol of the sanctity of labor. The brewer's tradition was kept alive through the Dark Ages largely by monasteries in Northern Europe, and the vintner's tradition was carried on by the monks of Southern Europe. For whiskey, we have Scottish and Irish monks to thank. If you doubt this, just look at all the saints whose names appear on the labels.

Central to the monastic tradition—which dates back to the 4th century AD and found its most harmonious form in the 5th century under St. Benedict—is the principle of "ora et labora," that is "prayer and labor." From early morning until late evening, the monk's day was divided into periods of work followed by periods of worship. This juxtaposition made work seem much more like prayer. (Judging from the record, it sometimes also made prayer seem more like work.)

Out of this joining of labor and prayer in Western tradition grew the notion of "vocation" which means simply "calling";

meaning that we are called to our work and called to a higher standard by a power greater than ourselves, the "mightiest worker of the universe," as Walter Rauschenbusch called God. Out of "ora et labora" also grew a sacred sense of justice and righteousness in the workplace which in time led to the abolition of slavery, the end of child labor, and better working conditions for workers across this nation. This time-honored principle is still active today in movements toward better working conditions and environmental awareness world-wide.

This close connection between worship and work, the sanctification of labor which was nurtured through the ages in monastic life, is in danger on several fronts. Now, increasingly, what used to be called "vocational" schools are called "technical" schools, which comes from the Greek "technikos" meaning simply "art" or "craft." The sense of calling, and thus the sense that work is holy, has fled and we are left with nothing to hold onto but technique.

The summer before I started seminary in 1966 I applied for a job as an overhead crane operator at the Abbott Iron Company (we called it the "Abbott and Costello Iron Company"), an old structural steel factory in a 200-foot-long building near Central Square in Cambridge, Massachusetts with machinery dating back at least to the 1940s. The boss, Mr. Abbott, interviewed me. Hat in hand, I told him I needed work and was going on to seminary in the Fall. He rolled his eyes as if to say, "I may be an abbot, but this is no place for a monk." Still, he was desperate, and I was desperate, so he hired me as an overhead crane operator. "Just don't tell anyone where you're going in the Fall," he said, "They'd never understand."

It turned out to be a great place to work. The foreman was a young African American man who would put his foot in the crane's huge hook and signal "UP" with his thumb so I could lift him high in the air and carry him from one end of the factory to the other. The other men were young and old, Italian, Mohawk,

Polish, and other, and all easy-going and good to each other. We liked each other. Over the next three months, I became a good crane operator, but I never once mentioned to anyone where I was going in the Fall.

When the Monday before Labor Day came around, I decided I was just plain going to tell them I was leaving soon and going on to seminary, and let the chips fall where they might. So I did. Instead of mocking me or being shocked, they expressed genuine sorrow that I was leaving and warmly wished me the best. I felt like a young man leaving a big Catholic family to enter the priesthood. The boss's fear of anything religious in the workplace was his own, not his workers'. They brought the sense of the holy into the factory on their own with their lunch-boxes, and blessed me with it, and sent a piece of their working holiness with me.

Jesus tells a stunning parable about a corrupt labor/management situation. A landlord rents out a vineyard with the reasonable understanding that the tenants will work the vineyard and take their rightful share of the produce, turning the rest over to the landlord who owns it all. Instead, the tenants take everything for themselves and give nothing to the owner. They even beat the owner's hired manager and kill the owner's son.

The disciples had no trouble understanding this parable about the danger of valuing our labor solely for what we can gain from it, while ignoring what others, God, and the Creation may gain or suffer from it. If our security, our benefits, our portfolio are the bottom line; if the Divine is excluded from our labors, then the whole workplace soon becomes debased and corrupt, and the workers are debased and corrupt as well. In the parable, the landlord evicts the selfish tenants and turns the vineyard over to tenants who are willing to serve others as well as themselves. This ought to make us take a hard look at our own labors.

In our day, so-called "market forces" are given a semi-divine status, with the Fed Chairman as their oracle. To point out the failings of the capitalist system is now tantamount to blasphemy.

To declare the truth that 20% of the children in the world's richest nation are living in poverty, or that we have a higher infant mortality rate and a poorer health care system than a score of smaller countries, is seen as sacrilege. Adam Smith's Invisible Hand, which supposedly apportions wealth to the few and withholds it from the many, is solemnly invoked as none other than the hand of the Almighty.

This is, of course, the rankest idolatry. God is not the author of any human economic system, whether it be capitalism, communism, socialism, or any other "-ism." We are always called to a higher standard. Without a higher standard, any economic system, like any person, will eventually become cruel, unjust and profane. Without a higher standard, work and worship will become strangers, then competitors, and then finally, enemies. Without a higher standard, we will soon find ourselves laboring in what William Blake calls "those Dark Satanic Mills."

Our national life today is dominated by titanic power struggles between big labor, big government, big corporations, big special interest groups, and big money. We are expected to give our ultimate allegiance and service, even our reverent devotion, to these great forces. We are asked to believe that there is no other power by which we need to govern our lives, and to forget that there is a power unimaginably greater, a power that crafted the original economy of the Cosmos that alone can restore wholeness, sanity, and sacredness to our work. That power is not to be found in servitude to labor, government, corporations or special interest groups. That power is before, behind, and above them all. That power is, simply, God. So, what can we do?

First, Hildegard of Bingen said, "Plant a garden, dig a ditch, toil and sweat... and offer this up to God as your true worship." If there is anything in our work that we cannot offer to God as true worship, then we need to change it fast. If your work is not true worship, then fire yourself, and find some work that is. I believe God will sustain you in this.

Second, if your bosses or co-workers are abusing the vineyard and violating standards of honesty and righteousness on the job, do not go along to get along. Call them firmly to a higher standard. If that does not work, then blow the whistle loud and shrill and prepare to leave. I believe from my own experience that God will sustain you in this, too.

Third, expect our labor leaders, our political leaders, our financial gurus to uphold a higher standard of justice and righteousness for all of the world's workers. Why should we not expect that their work, and our own, be real worship? Why should we not expect that justice be done for the poor, the weak, the silent, the old, and the forgotten?

If we do not do these things; if our work is a rebuke to righteousness and a rejection of justice, then the vineyard will be taken from us, and given to those whose labor is sanctified by the Big Boss, the Great Economist of the Cosmos. If we do these things, we will be sustained, and the fruits of our labor will be finer than we ever dreamed. *Ora et Labora*, Prayer and Labor, Worship and Work. The way has been shown to us for ages. Now, it is for us to follow.

Fall

HUNTING SEASON

With the coming of Fall, hunting season begins as it has since the dawn of humanity. When I was a young man, I did a good deal of varmint hunting, and was a pretty good shot, winning marksmanship awards and all that. But, I killed my first and last deer one dark night in Northern Wisconsin where I was an 18-year-old foreman at a summer resort. That night our supper was interrupted with the news that a deer had been struck by a car and lay fallen, but alive, in the road. I rushed outside with the only rifle we had: a .22 loaded with long rifle shells. The deer was a doe and her hind legs were both broken. She was suffering, and it was my job to dispatch her. I did the job, but it was a long and agonizing ordeal. I can still vividly see, hear and smell the whole scene more than 40 years later. That was enough for me. I never killed another deer.

Today, there seems to be some fear among hunters that their ancient craft may be threatened. Every year, it seems, fewer hunting licenses are issued. The conventional wisdom says that the coming generation is too hooked on video games and too soft to handle the rigors of hunting. Another fear is that so-called "anti-hunters" are bent on eliminating hunting all over the country by political pressure. The recent referendum on bear-baiting in Maine is held up as an example. These theories of why hunting is becoming a lost art may or may not be true.

Here are some other thoughts. One look at the Fall catalog from Cabela's, the self-styled "World's Greatest Outfitter," reveals that the fully-equipped hunter today must have hundreds, if not thousands of dollars worth of equipment: plastic rattling antlers at $22.99, deer calls at up to $40 or $100 for the electronic calls, special clothing that masks human scent at several hundred dollars, a digital trail camera at $350, your GPS so you don't get lost at up to $400, automated feeding stations to attract the game with seductive aromas and sweet treats, carts to haul the carcass, laser-sighted scopes at well over $1000, and much more high-tech equipment.

An informal calculation is that a deer or bear which dresses out at say 80 pounds taken with this sort of equipment could cost the hunter $80-$100 per pound of meat. Add in the four-wheel-drive pick-up and the ATV to get the high-tech hunter out there where the game is without all that arduous hiking into the williwags and hauling out of the carcass, and the cost of your meat approaches hundreds of dollars a pound. Hello. What happened to the simple economy of the hunt? What happened to the stark beauty of the fair chase and the nearly even matching of wits and physical prowess between man and animal? What happened to the skills of woodsmanship, tracking, and finding the way in the wilderness without all the expensive high-tech gear?

If you want to know why the hunter—not the deer, the duck, the moose or the bear, but the plain, old-fashioned good hunter—may be an endangered species, just check out the hunting catalogs. Think about it.

ROAD KILL

Fair warning: this piece starts harsh; but it finishes fine. In Autumn—along with the sadness of the end of summer, the falling leaves and the dying of the old year—there is the sadness of the dying of so many young creatures on the roads. Mostly the yearlings of mammals, we see them by the scores—squirrels, porcupines, raccoons skunks, beavers, foxes, even a marten—curled up as though sleeping peacefully on the shoulder, or pounded into pemmican on the pavement. To some, this is a source of amusement. We've seen the menus for mythical Road-kill Restaurants listing Rack of 'Coon, Skunk Steak, or Beaver Burger. I once wrote an oft-requested song about Road-Kill Billy, who found his food on the Interstate. The dark humor masks the shame we feel at seeing young creatures, whose faces and forms grace children's books and wild-life calendars, destroyed as collateral damage to our ruthless crusade for comfort, convenience and velocity. It is like the mordant humor of soldiers through the ages, mocking the death of others, knowing that their own death could come just as blindly and suddenly. Every time we speed past our dead four-legged cousins—so like us genetically—we have to harden our hearts to such senseless slaughter just to keep on driving. This endangers our souls. Some tender hearts attach to their vehicles little whistles supposed to emit a high-pitched warning to let the little ones know that a ton of steel is hurtling blindly toward them at a mile a minute. We hope they work. Some tough guys try to hit the little wanderers on the way, or so we're told. We hope they don't. "God's eye is on the sparrow, and I know He watches me."

What to do? Several things: First, drive less and slower. This makes good sense for many reasons. Second, most of these creatures are nocturnal; so, if you have to drive at night, don't out-drive your headlights. Stay at 45 m.p.h. or less, and be alert for the lights of their eyes shining in the dark. Third, keep a shovel and gloves in the back of your vehicle and, if traffic allows, remove the dead from the road and respectfully bury them, or at least put them on the living soil so that they can return quickly to life. Say a prayer for them. This will save those who follow on the road from the pain of seeing such carnage, and it will also show the spirit of the creature and the Creator that someone cares. Of course, if you have the stomach for it, you could take them home and respectfully put them to good use for food or fur, making something beautiful from something horrible. Don't cry. Don't curse. Just care.

When I am very old, perhaps I'll found an order of pilgrims who will amble along the roads to do the right thing by these fresh-fallen fellow creatures, and teach others to do the same. Maybe we'll call it the Order of Crow & Raven. As the beasts of the field teach us how to respect their young, we can learn to respect the young of our own species, and stop hardening our hearts to the death of any of them, anywhere, anytime, for any reason.

Here is a prayer I use for any fallen creature: "All our relatives, all living things, see this one who has fallen. See this one who lately walked the fields and busied himself with small things. All our relatives, hold her. Let her not be out of life long."

Maybe you'll tape this to your dashboard and say use it. It could make you feel better.

LATE BLOOMERS

We're noticing many late bloomers in the fields below Blue Hill Mountain, 'Awanadjo' in Algonkian. There are the expected Autumn flowers, of course, like the goldenrods and the asters, but there are also some remarkable Spring and early Summer flowers surprisingly and boldly blooming again now, enjoying a last fling into Fall. We've seen lupines in bloom this past week, not a lot, but enough to catch the eye with their purple, pink and white spires, rising above the browning fields far past their usual June season. The yellow hawkweed and red clover, both early summer flowers, are boldly blooming again here and there. We also saw some mind-boggling blossoms of bluets, a very early Spring flower, in our sojourns this past quarter moon. We've even seen blueberry bushes blooming in the snows of late October.

This brings to mind some remarkable cases of late-blooming among our own species. An 88-year-old woman of very hardy stock, after many days of lying in bed, breathing her last and not even knowing her only child, sat up and had breakfast, recognized family members, smiled, returned to her bed and died. A 90-year-old captain and ship-model-builder, also on his death-bed, got up and with steady hand repaired a broken boom on one of his models before returning to his bed to arise no more. A 96-year-old lady also of rugged stock who had lain on her death-bed for many days, suddenly decided she wanted to get up and go for a ride. She had dinner at the home of friends, admiring the view and enjoying the company and the conversation until it was time to return to the nursing home where she died within a day.

Of course, these things all happened in and around Blue Hill, which is a remarkable place in one man's opinion, but the earth is a remarkable place, and late-blooming is surely a world-wide phenomenon. Look at Grandma Moses who became a widely recognized folk artist in her 80s. Buckminster Fuller and Bertrand Russell achieved their greatest recognition in their 90s. Look at Robert Frost and Carl Sandburg. "Granny D" Doris Haddock walked across the country in her 90s to call attention to campaign finance corruption. Then, there's the folk-tale of a late-blooming Winston Churchill in his far 80s struggling up from his chair to give a commencement address at a midwestern college, gripping the podium and delivering these words: "Never give up. Never give up. Never give up."

There are countless late-bloomers of every species, type, variety, sort and kind out there bringing hope and unexpected beauty into a weary world. It's never too late. As long as there are a few warm coals in the stove, the fire can roar again. As long as there a few slumbering seeds, the fields and forests are not dead. The eagle, the loon, the moose, the turkey, the beaver, the cougar, the wolf have all come back from the edge of extinction. Lazarus rose from the grave. So did Jesus, to bring a whole new hope into being.

VETERANS DAY

Veteran's Day, formerly called Armistice Day marks the November 11, 1918 end of World War I, "The War to End All Wars." Conservative estimates of loss of life in that war are around 10 million combatants and 20 million civilians, for a total of 30 million victims. This war did not end all wars, of course. It was soon followed by World War II: rough estimates are another 30 million dead including the 6 million civilians who died in the Holocaust and a half million who died at Hiroshima and Nagasaki. An estimate for the Korean War would be roughly two million.

The culture wars of Josef Stalin took an estimated 20 million, nearly all civilians. Next we had Mao's culture wars: conservative estimate possibly 20 million dead, nearly all civilians. The Vietnam War left 56,000 Americans and 1 million Vietnamese dead, followed by Pol Pot's culture wars in Cambodia killing an estimated 2 million civilians. The Rwandan genocide killed close to one million, again mostly civilians. Then, to wrap up the 20th century, Gulf War I and ten years of sanctions in Iraq causing death from malnourishment and lack of medical care particularly among children, left one million dead. I am sure I have missed a few wars and few million deaths here and there. I am not a demographer or political scientist, but it should be clear to anyone that World War I did not end all wars. A conservative estimate for deaths in all wars in the 20th century might be about 120 million, the vast majority being non-combatants. This amounts to 1.2 million deaths a year.

Now, if a great plague of disease were running rampant across the world claiming 100,000 victims a month for a hundred years, do we not think that every medical researcher, doctor, chemist, public health official, every pharmaceutical firm, every major university and every government would be making a monumental effort to overcome such a scourge, such a deadly epidemic taking the lives of men, women and children world-wide?

Yet, what do we do? We shake our heads, cluck our tongues, wave our flags, sing our national anthems, weep, lay flowers on graves, and make excuses and justifications. What is more, we Americans, you and I, pay out of pocket nearly a trillion dollars every year for more weapons and wars, with hardly a complaint, while millions of Americans are hungry and lack medical care and our bridges collapse and our highways crumble. You can still be thrown in prison for non-violent opposition to war, even in America. Or, you may simply be written off as a foolish, starry-eyed, sappy, pollyannish, liberal idealist with no grasp of *realpolitik*.

It is not that we do not know how to stop wars before they start. Diplomacy, mediation, cooperation, sanctions, international law and treaties have all proven effective in the past. But the rush to mass violence by ambitious, aggressive, self-aggrandizing leaders who do not put their own lives on the line still goes on. Is your leadership being criticized? Is your approval rating sinking in the polls? Start a war and everyone falls silent and follows meekly along, sending their children and their hard-earned money to feed the mechanisms of mass violence.

It reminds me of the man who said, "I am was so upset last night that I just wanted to ask God why he would allow such suffering and dying in the world, but I decided not to ask."

"Why in heaven not?" said his companion.

The man answered, "Because I was afraid God would ask me the same question."

So on this Veteran's Day, who are the veterans we honor? They are those who have endured the hardships of war. First we remember the soldier who has volunteered to fight, risked injury or death, and returned a hero. He is the one we honor with flags and medals and memorials. He chose to go, and we honor him.

Yet there are many other veterans through the ages who are not so honored. They were captives or slaves or poor or children or beaten men who made war unwillingly to avoid starvation or prison or execution by sword or hanging or firing squad. Are they not veterans worthy of memory?

There were the Quakers and Mennonites, Buddhists and Jehovah's Witnesses, the pacifists who for reasons of faith or conscience endured scorn and prison and death rather than fight in wars they abhorred. Are they not veterans of the hardships and cruelties of war, to be honored for their courage?

What of those who fought in unpopular wars and returned home to be disdained by their neighbors and forgotten by the government they served? Are they not veterans too? Consider our children and grandchildren who will be sorely burdened with the costs of our present wars for years to come. Will they not be veterans of the brutality of war?

Most of all, what of the millions upon millions of innocent women, children, the elderly and infirm through the ages from Jericho to Wounded Knee to Auschwitz to Nagasaki to Fallujah who wanted nothing of war, wanted nothing but to care for their own in peace, when war suddenly stormed into their village to plunder and pillage or fell from the sky to blast and burn? Are these innocents not true veterans too? Did they not make the ultimate sacrifice on the altar of war? Shall we not honor them?

So we honor the one veteran and not the others. Why? Because he was willing to kill or be killed, willing to choose death over life. Alas for him, and for all of us. The scripture says, "I have set before thee life and death... Therefore choose life that thou and thy seed may live."

If we are to honor the veterans of war, let's honor them all: weak and strong, willing and unwilling, living and dead, for they have all suffered the cruel and fruitless disasters of war. They are all veterans of war.

And all victims.

HOMELAND SECURITY

We know that tourist season is over when we no longer hear the call of the vehicle security system. Mostly, local people do not lock their cars when they go into the bank or Merrill & Hinckley's store because we know each other and are vigilant, and because locals usually don't drive tempting high-end vehicles loaded with gadgets anyway. Many still do not lock their houses at night. We don't lock the church. We've tried, but everyone has a key or can find their way in if they really want to. Someone stole a silver-plate communion pitcher a few years back, but it turned up on the doorstep with an anonymous confessional note attached a while later. One of our teachers said, "Lay not up for yourselves treasure on earth where moth and rust corrupt and thieves break in and steal. Lay up for yourselves treasure in heaven..."

Our nation has spent billions in treasure on homeland security. Meanwhile, *Time* magazine reports that, while little old ladies are searched and scanned on the way to visit the grandkids, over 4,000 people walk freely across our southern border everyday. *Time* also estimates that in one year nearly 200,000 non-Mexicans from Central and South America, Asia and the

Middle East walked into the US without even a tip of the hat to homeland security.

There is a physical law at work in this immigration business. It's called "osmosis," which you may remember from high school, whereby particles will move from a solution of greater concentration to one of lesser concentration or the reverse, until stability is reached. The poor will always move from places of greater poverty to places of lesser poverty, just as our ancestors did. Someone asked Willy Sutton, "Why do you rob banks?" He answered, "Because that's where the money is." Why did Robin Hood poach deer in the king's forest? Because that's where the meat was. This law also applies to weapons of mass destruction. If some countries have nuclear, chemical and biological weapons, other countries will get them too, by hook or by crook, for their own homeland security.

Call it Osmosis. Call it The Law of Robin Hood. Call it what you want, but as long as the king has plenty of deer while others are hungry, poaching will flourish. Hang ten poachers and a hundred will spring up to replace them. As long as some have weapons of mass destruction, others will try to get them. You can decimate Iraq; but Iran, Pakistan, India, North Korea, China, and others will take their place. The late James Russell Wiggins, lifelong Democrat, former UN ambassador, editor of the Washington Post and the Ellsworth American, said to me shortly before his death at 95, "Rob, the United States is in a perfect position to end the threat of nuclear war right now, by destroying its atomic weapons and insisting that everyone do the same. We've got to do it before it's too late."

What is homeland security? So long as some have weapons of mass destruction while others do not, so long as some have decent schools while others have none, so long as some have medical care while others are suffering unattended, so long as some are obese while others are starving, so long as some drive everywhere while others walk with their worldly goods in trash bags on their backs, so long as some live in huge trophy houses while others live under plastic tarps; you can spend your millions or billions or trillions, but there will be no homeland security: Not for you, not for me, not for anyone.

THE BIBLE

bags on their back so long as some have to have trophy houses while others live under plastic tarps... you can spend your coupons or billions or trillions... and the end will be financial security... Not for you, not for me, not for anyone.

The Bible still provides the first language for Westerners to talk about the spiritual life. It is like the software for finding our place in the created cosmos, and interfacing with it. It is also the fountainhead of so much of our history and literature. Just try to imagine the works of Shakespeare, Milton, Blake, Jefferson, Lincoln, Churchill, Dr. King or any of the great voices of Western history and literature without Biblical themes. Try to imagine 20 centuries of Western art without visual images from the Bible.

Moreover, the Bible has always been the primary handbook for change, revolution and justice. The passion to make the Bible available to all people in their native tongue fed the first democratic revolutionary movements in Europe in the 15th and 16th centuries and led to the invention of the printing press and the ideas of freedom of speech and the press. It is impossible to imagine the reforming work of the Abolitionists, Jane Addams, Dorothy Day, Eleanor Roosevelt, Martin Luther King, Mother Teresa or Desmond Tutu without the Biblical mandate for justice.

No person can claim to be educated and be unfamiliar with the Bible. It is still the best-selling book in the world (managing to stay ahead of even the "Left Behind" series). It is a unique record of the human/divine dialog in good times and bad, over four millennia. A practicing Christian (and we are all just practicing, 'til we get it right) will have an active engagement with the Bible.

There is a very simple way to read the Bible that has worked over the centuries, and works today for seekers and the curious everywhere. Keep a Bible with two markers in it—one for the Old Testament, and one for the New. Read some in the morning and some in the evening. Start with the table of contents. Then, read one Psalm daily, listening to the voice of the Psalmist weeping or giving thanks. In Autumn, read Genesis and Exodus. After Thanksgiving, read Isaiah, Jeremiah and other prophets until Christmas. At Christmas read the first chapters of Matthew and Luke out loud. After Christmas, choose one gospel—Matthew, Mark, Luke or John—and read it all the way through, chapter by chapter, through Lent, finishing at Easter.

In the Spring, read Acts, Song of Solomon, and maybe one of the minor prophets—like Micah or Joel. In the Summer read the letters of Paul or anything else that appeals to you, because it is Summer, after all. When you get tired of God-talk, read Proverbs or Ecclesiastes. If you want the Old Testament in a nut-shell, read Amos or Joel. If you want the New Testament in a nut-shell, read Mark and James. If you're feeling hopeless, read Isaiah. If you're feeling like the ruler of the world, read Job, Ecclesiastes or Revelation. It's all there.

When you are in trouble or wondering what to do next, do open the Bible. Never mind the liberal disdain for such things. You will be amazed at how the scripture will speak to you if you'll engage it. When someone with whom you agree—or disagree—cites scripture, look it up, for pity's sake! It is surprising how people interpret the same passages differently. And, most important; every time you read in the Bible, read it as though for the first time—all fresh, new news. Bring nothing to it, not your past, not your parents or teachers or preachers. Hear it just as it is. You will not be disappointed: shocked, surprised, inspired maybe, but not disappointed. Read it until it is yours. This will take some time, but why not? Shall we only read the *New York Times* or the *Wall Street Journal*, or the *Bangor Daily News*, or watch Fox or CNN and consider ourselves in touch? Better to get in touch with our ancient heritage.

Why? There are always those who would impose their own interpretation of scripture on everyone else. You have heard TV preachers do it. You have heard politicians and aspiring politicians—both liberal and conservative—do it. But, the Bible is not their book. It is everyone's book—if we will simply read it. That is what the heretics and reformers died for. The problem is that we have given up this central document of our spiritual heritage to those with a very particular agenda.

Burton Throckmorton, late professor of New Testament, said this:

"We dare not take the Bible for granted. We seem to suppose it will always be there when we want it, when we need it—but will it? Or will we allow ourselves to float so far away from it, from our moorings, that we will have forgotten how to read it and will not be able to know any more what it says? What we are doing now, however, is letting the fundamentalists take the Bible, letting them be its sole interpreters, letting them tell everyone what it means. The danger is that we will be embarrassed or ashamed to quote it, to be seen reading or studying it; but those of us who are non-fundamentalist Christians cannot give up our claim to the Bible."

I will add what Dr. Throckmorton was perhaps too diplomatic to say. Many of us have given up the Bible because it demands too much of us, both in terms of faith and of action. For example, the Ten Commandments present no objections to homosexual behavior, nor does Jesus, though both prohibit adultery. On the other hand, the Levitical code and the Apostle Paul both prohibit some—but not all— homosexual behaviors as they do some—but not all—heterosexual behaviors: like adultery again.

So, when conservatives seek on Biblical grounds to explicitly exclude homosexuals from rights that others enjoy, but do not explicitly exclude adulterers, they are being hypocritical, and do not have a Biblical leg to stand on. When liberals—on the grounds that the Bible teaches the sanctity of human life—condemn war or capital punishment, but do not condemn abortion or assisted suicide or embryonic stem cell research, they too are being hypocritical, in this preacher's view.

The Bible makes some hard demands upon us. To ease the hardness of those demands, we are inclined to either throw out the Bible all together, or throw out those parts that are disagreeable to us while loudly proclaiming the divine truth of those parts which are agreeable. Those who interpret scripture liberally tend to put more weight on collective sins and demands for justice for the poor and the weak, while winking at individual sins. Those who interpret scripture conservatively tend to put more weight on individual sins and prohibitions against certain personal behaviors, while ignoring collective ones. It reminds me of the old saw about the difference between Republicans and Democrats: Republicans pull their window shades down when there is really no need to, and Democrats leave them up when they should really pull them down.

If we will face it with open mind and open heart, get directly with it, and stop forcing it to meet our own needs—the Bible can be our guide, comforter, inspiration, judge, coach, challenger, and friend. If we are open to it, we are not guaranteed an easy alliance, or a perfect union, anymore than we are when we open ourselves to another person. We are not guaranteed convenience and ease, nor an endorsement of our sins and a condemnation of the sins of others. But we *are* guaranteed a timeless communion with those who came before us, with those who are now seeking, and with the Source, the Word by Whose will, desire, and love, we all came into being, and Who will likewise receive us lovingly in the fullness of time.

THE PREACHER

Like it or not, when a person takes up preaching, even old friends may stop seeing a person and start seeing a preacher instead. The role may overwhelm the soul. Some preachers will work to preserve their true selves; others will gladly let the role rule.

I find that people, often without being aware of it, project onto the minister their own images of what a holy person should resemble. Why are so many people curious about what the minister is buying at the store, combining a smiling greeting with a surreptitious glance into his or her shopping bucket? Do they wonder what holy people eat and drink? Why do people carefully watch their language while talking to the minister, or apologize ("excuse my French") for using certain words, whether they bother the minister or not? Perhaps it is because the minister is seen as pure and undefiled; in some sense, holy.

A minister may also be seen as a scapegoat. This is largely due to the fact that he or she is highly visible. If a church is having troubles, it may be easier to blame the minister than to look deeply at the root causes which may be much more complex. Or if an individual is having troubles, the minister may be subject to accusations that he or she doesn't call enough, or is insensitive, or is too ideological, or not ideological enough, or too passive or too domineering. Truth is; we make good targets. After all, we put our heads up and sound off every week and everyone knows where to find us.

The minister may be seen as a shaman—one who has mysterious powers and can call down blessings or curses, or even influence natural events. How many times have I heard, "Put in a good word for me with the Man Upstairs, will you...? You know, the Big Guy?" (And here I thought the big guy was Goliath... or maybe Jesse Ventura.)

I am not a holy person. I am not a magician. I am not a sterling example of conduct or industry or commitment or love. Ordination did not make me better, though in some ways it made me different, with a different field in which to sin or shine, forgive and be forgiven. Ordination does not adhere to a person like a cockleburr, but can only be conferred by a congregation. A minister without a congregation is not a minister, just as a woman without a husband is not a wife or a man without a wife is not a husband.

Coming from a business background, a person may wonder why the church is not run like a business with the minister as a manager or CEO. Coming from a military background, a person may wonder why the minister is not a commander. There are precious few roles in a secular society in the 21st century that call for the exercise of sacred power. One of the few is that of the small town pastor.

The pastor may be seen as the local seer or magus with visionary gifts. I have seen brawny fishermen turn pale when I walked into their hospital room. They were wondering what I knew that they didn't. I have seen the distress in face of someone who thought I could descry without being told when someone was sick or in the hospital or needed a home visit. I have heard the father of the bride say, "We'd like to have some good weather for the wedding tomorrow, Reverend," enough times to know that preachers may be assumed to have greater powers in certain realms than, say, the first selectman or the fire chief.

The shaman also has influence over malign powers. One evening I got a call from a lady who'd been to church a few times. She said, "My husband has had a heart attack and is down at the hospital." I said, "Oh, I'd be glad to go down and visit him." "Oh, no," she said, "He's not much for church. But my daughter and I are here alone and there is a bat in the house. Could you come over and get it out?" And I did, but not by any supernatural powers.

When I arrived mother and daughter were huddled in one bed. Just a coffee can and a piece of cardboard were all that it took to perform the necessary magic of making a bat disappear, to the delighted clucking of the ladies, after which I bowed and backed out the door.

Since sacred power—like the *mana* of the South Pacific, or the *manitou* of North America—can be benign or malign, great care is required for the benevolent exercise of that power. Like fire or electricity, sacred power can be dangerous. I do not exaggerate here. One danger a pastor faces is assuming that the power lies primarily within him- or herself. This illusion may be encouraged by modern theological education which is inclined toward imparting sacred knowledge. This implies that the source of sacred power is the possession of the correct sort of 'head' knowledge.

Sacred power proceeds from the tradition, nature, God and other people. It comes from all directions, not just from within. It is not so much to be boldly taken as it is accepted with a measure of fear and humility. To lose sight of this may lead to the willful seizing and exercise of individual power resulting in damage far and wide, or simply in the inability to exercise any power at all.

Another danger is that the pastor will operate under the illusion that sacred power is primarily exercised through spoken language. This is refuted by the pastor who is not a powerful preacher but is still very able to use sacred power to change lives at critical times: deaths, marriages, personal crises, spiritual crises and the like. It is also refuted by the fine preacher whose life is dissonant with the preaching, thus debasing the preaching and rendering it, in the end, malignant. There are countless examples of exalted preachers who have fallen this way, from Henry Ward Beecher to Ted Haggard. Eventually, the walk unfailingly speaks louder than the talk.

Sacred power proceeds from traditional scripture and liturgy. They are sources of power as shown in the uses of this power for good in the lives and circumstances of our forebears. If they didn't work, they would not have been handed down to us. The memory and history of times when this sacred power has resulted in healing and harmony enable us to recall and create a like result. I think of the powers of traditional prayer and song applied to the civil rights movement and other reform movements, when the word became flesh, and preaching became social reform.

Traditional sacred music is also a great source of spiritual power often neglected in theological education. To know sacred music, to play an instrument, to be able to sing—regardless of how well—can be a major channel for the movement of sacred power into worship and life. Particularly in times of conflict, sacred music can bring people together in ways that scripture, preaching and liturgy cannot. There have been times when we resorted to singing *Blessed Be the Tie that Binds* to marvelously bring us together again after a fractious congregational meeting.

Of course, there are also historical examples of the malignant exercise of scriptural and liturgical tradition, including endless wars between Protestants and Catholics, and violence between Sunnis and Shiites.

A corollary to this is that power also proceeds from the traditions of the place in which the pastor serves. Churches and towns have their own traditions including cooperation or rivalries between churches, ways of helping those in crisis, public functions like Christmas, Easter, Memorial Day, July 4th and the like. It is good to understand these as occasions for the exercise of either benevolent or malign spiritual power.

Sacred power also proceeds from Nature because, despite dire predictions of the end of Nature, Nature herself is still far beyond human control. It has been my great good fortune to live in a place and among people where the powers of Nature are deeply respected and honored.

Benign sacred power is power exercised for the good of all. Malign spiritual power is power exercised for the good of the individual or a particular party. To exercise such power on behalf of a particular denomination or doctrine or dogma is to lose the power, or worse, to do harm. To rightly exercise sacred power, the pastor must do so for the health of the whole community. That community embraces the pastor, the church, the town, the land surrounding, and the whole seamless earth. To exercise power for anything less is to deny the sacred, and risk severe judgment.

NO DISTINCTIONS

March 2008

Dear Athanasius,

Many thanks for taking the time yesterday to meet with me and express your serious and heartfelt concerns about our church, our worship and my leadership. It's refreshing when someone is up front about these things instead of just grumbling in the background.

I didn't fully respond to you on the spot because I prefer to listen and then ponder a little before I try to put it into words. So I will try to do that now. The model of pastoral leadership I prefer is collaborative and consensual—working together after agreement on goals and methods has been reached. This model can be very effective in a group with many high-powered people as in our church. Instead of trying to overpower them, it attempts to empower them. I am quite aware that this model can be confusing and even infuriating to some who are not accustomed to it.

It is my sense that sometimes you and I have worked very

well together and other times, not so well. For the latter, I take my full share of the responsibility. I may have been too haughty or impatient or did not fully explain my viewpoint, as I am trying to do now. I may have dragged my feet. I also may have hindered in other ways of which I am unaware. For that I am sorry.

As I mentioned yesterday, I get my model of leadership from my family (two brothers, father, mother, grandfather all clergy). But it is also deeply rooted in my understanding of the gospel; that is, that we are equal in the eyes of God regardless of our gifts: intellectual or artistic, spiritual or material.

The pyramid model you describe suggests to me, perhaps incorrectly, that the leader will pay more attention to those who have greater gifts, particularly material gifts. This creates an implicit hierarchy within the congregation, with the many at the base of the pyramid not as essential to the body as the few at the top. This runs counter to my gut understanding of the gospel which is that Jesus did not make such distinctions and we are not to do so either (James 2:1-7). My understanding is that Jesus set that pyramid on its point, saying that the first shall be last and the last first (Mark 10:42-44 et. al.). I know this sounds preachy, but I'm a preacher.

To the often-heard charge that you can't run an organization that way, my response is that we are called to keep trying until we can. During my watch our congregation has weathered several serious storms within and without and, thanks to all its dedicated members, managed to pay the bills, keep the buildings and programs sound, and, most important, remain a fine and able vessel of spirit, charity and creativity in our community.

My goal, like yours, is to leave the place a little better than I found it. There is another serious storm coming for all of us, and I am hopeful that we can weather it too, if we are willing to pull together and not pull apart. If the time comes when you and I are working together again, I will welcome it wholeheartedly.

Sincerely...

(This letter unfortunately did not close the widening rift between me and the addressee. However, I am still hopeful.)

PREDESTINATION

In Calvinist theology, predestination in its purest form is the doctrine that we can do nothing in this life to determine our destiny in the next. Predestination is another demonstration of the futility of humans trying to unscrew the inscrutable, or understand the 'mind of God.' Yes, this doctrine has many flaws and inconsistencies. For example, it consigns some saints to eternal damnation, and some scoundrels to paradise. Why? Because God said so. On the face of it, this may present the image of a cold, cruel God who cares not what we do or believe, and condemns the good and the bad alike. But, there may be some good effects of this concept on our living of this present life.

First and foremost, predestination declares that we can have no foreknowledge of, or control over, what will happen to us after we die. This surely matches our experience. Once I am dead, God is in charge of my destiny. Predestination suggests that these matters are out of our hands and entirely in God's hands, and we would best turn our attention to this life, not the next. This means that we may or may not be saved by our good works, or our faith, or attendance at church, or the repeating of creeds or liturgical formulas. We cannot know how we are destined.

We cannot, further, know how others are destined. We cannot judge others as saved or damned in God's scheme of things. These are mysteries known to God alone. We don't even get a peek. Someone once said that there are two surprises when you go to heaven. One is the surprise at who is not there that we expected would be. The other is the surprise at who is there that we expected would not. (Your preacher humbly—and heretically—suggests there may be a third surprise: that there is no heaven, or hell as we've always believed.)

Predestination means that we do the right thing in this life purely because it is the right thing to do, not for some selfish motive, or because it guarantees us eternal bliss, or because it will save someone else, or even save the world. We do good simply to do good. It means that we are not called to judge who will go to heaven and who to hell, but simply to love God and one another, because we cannot know about heaven and hell. It means that we work and pray for the good it will bring to others and to the Creation, not for any points that we might cash in on the other side of Jordan.

This calls for us to lose ourselves in selfless effort for the Creation, with less thought for our own salvation either now or later. It removes from human understanding and control the dynamics of salvation or of the next life, and turns our heads to the improving of this present life for ourselves and others. It emphasizes the limited nature of human knowledge and effort, and calls us to greater faith in the infinitely wise and unknown purposes of God, whose ways are not our ways, and whose thoughts are not our thoughts.

In short, the ancient and oft-maligned concept of predestination may offer a liberation from the ritualistic practices of organized religion and a simple, wholistic call to do good to all creatures in this world for the sake of doing good, with no desire of, or claim for, reward in this life or the next.

THE NEW ATHEISM

There are some serious challenges to faith in the 21st century. First, there is the merchandising of faith. 'Christian' amusement parks, music, books, films, electric ceramic nativity scenes, 'Jesus Loves Me' coffee mugs, T-shirts, jewelry, key-chains, and other paraphernalia now amount to a multi-billion dollar industry. Unfortunately, the standards of merchandising often run counter to the standards of our faith tradition. To sell songs and trinkets implying that they will somehow magically enhance our spirituality or our salvation was once seen as an evil; it was called idolatry or 'simony' in the early church. The Protestant Reformation was ignited by the selling of indulgences for the false forgiveness of sins, in place of the ancient practices of personal confession, repentance and making amends. We're overdue for another reformation in the business of Christian merchandising, and that includes politics.

Another challenge to 21st century faith is heard in the trumpeting tantrums of Literalism coming both from the Right and from the Left. It might not be so bad if they could play the trumpet with a little joy or grace or soul.

"But wait a minute, you don't mean 'literalism' on the Left, do you?" asks a liberal in the back row. Yes. On the Right, of course, literalism trumpets in favor of language about the virgin birth, the divinity of Christ, and the fearsome visions of judgment in the book of Revelation. On the Left, literalism trumpets against language about God as Father and Jesus as Lord, and bowdlerizes the words of historic hymns and statements of faith rather than taking them for what they are: figurative, poetic language. Both the Left and the Right are blinded by literalism.

Since we're the salt of the earth; maybe we can just take all of this wrangling over language with a grain of salt, like poet/preacher John Donne in his "Devotions Upon Emergent Occasions" (1624)

"My God, my God, thou art a direct God, may I not say a literal God, a God that woulds't be understood literally and according to the plain sense of all thou sayest... But thou art also... a figurative... God too; a God in whose words are such a height of figures, such voyages, such peregrinations to fetch remote and precious metaphors, such extensions, such spreadings, such curtains of allegories, such third heavens of hyperboles, so harmonious elocutions, so retired and so reserved expressions, so commanding persuasions, so persuading commandments, such sinews even in thy milk."

Another challenge to faith in the 21ˢᵗ century is the wholesale rejection of ancient spiritual traditions in favor of one or another human ideology, for example, secularism, individualism, nihilism, scientism, or rationalism. But, according to G.K. Chesterton, "The opposite of believing in something is not believing in nothing, it is believing in anything." Or, as the Qur'an puts it, "If a man has no teacher, the Devil becomes his teacher." There is much to be gained by using the language and imagery of traditional religion without being bound by traditional dogma, but, by throwing out the whole body of spiritual tradition, the wisdom of the centuries, we risk throwing out the proverbial baby with the bath.

It is good to remember that there is *faith*, meaning "the conviction of things hoped for and the assurance of things unseen" according to the letter to the Hebrews, but there are also *faiths*, meaning particular religious faiths, doctrines and dogmas. Faiths being the work of men, rise and fall, come and go, but faith, being the work of God, remains forever. We are gathered here with faith far more than in any particular faith. There is a powerful difference.

The rejection of faith traditions in the name of reason or rationalism has recently enjoyed quite a boom. Richard Dawkins's book, *The God Delusion*, was for many weeks on the New York Times bestseller list with this summary: "An Oxford scientist asserts that belief in God is irrational and that religion has done great harm to the world." Who could argue with this? But of course, the same assertions could be made about science and technology which gave us weapons of mass destruction, the collapse of world fisheries, and global climate change, among other things. The same assertions could, in fact, be made about the entire human race: that they are irrational and that they have done a great deal of harm to the world. What would Prof. Dawkins have us do? Abolish religion? Or science and technology? Or the human race?

More striking is Sam Harris's *The End of Faith*, a huge bestseller which asserted that beliefs may be inherently dangerous. Harris writes, "Some propositions are so dangerous that it may even be ethical to kill people for believing them... Certain beliefs place their adherents beyond any peaceful means of persuasion." Harris is referring, of course, to Muslims, but I find his proposition dangerous in itself. I had thought—perhaps naively—that what we so earnestly call 'Western Civilization' had progressed beyond suggesting that people should be killed for their beliefs, but there it is on page 52 in *The End of Faith*. These men may be far more intelligent than I, but they cannot convince me because, in my opinion, their intellect has devoured their soul. Far from denying faith, they are actually displaying a blind and unfounded faith in human reason.

Belief in undefined human 'Reason' is no more verifiable than belief in 'God.' Yes, horrible things have been done by those who marched over the broken, bleeding bodies of others under the flag of religion: the Crusades, the Conquistadores, the Inquisition, mass persecutions of the Jews, the Salem witch trials. But horrible things have also been done by those who marched over the bleeding bodies of others under the flag of anti-religion: the Reign of Terror in France, the Nazi holocaust, Stalin's starvations, Mao's revolution, Pol Pot's killing fields. It is neither the flag of Faith nor the flag of Reason that is horrible; it is the marching over the broken, bleeding bodies of others under any flag or no flag at all that is horrible.

Faith and Reason are both God-given and must work together. Reason is not a substitute for Faith, nor is Faith a substitute for Reason. Faith without Reason is helpless, and Reason without Faith is heartless. Faith forges ahead into the unknown after Reason has reached its limits. They are not enemies. They need each other.

If faith alone, or reason alone, do not make a better world, then they have failed. The test of both faith and reason is to promote justice, righteousness, and peace to redeem the world from destruction. Justice means uniform standards of human law, equal rights to life, liberty and property, food, clothing and shelter, and the same freedoms for every human being. Righteousness means personal morality, decency, fidelity, integrity, commitment, responsibility, right livelihood, love for neighbor and God. Peace means stability, security, absence of fear, refusal to employ violence except as the very last resort. It means, in the words of Isaiah, that we "shall not raise our children for calamity."

The Gospel truth is that neither faith nor reason can redeem the world until they are animated by love. Love is simply desiring the good for our loved ones, and wanting for everyone what we want for our own. Yes, love is an emotion, the most powerful emotion: stronger than fear or hate. Love casts out fear, and overwhelms hate. Love is deeper than reason. Consider the animals: they may or may not reason, but they do love. But love must be expressed and acted out in rational, reasonable ways or it will fail.

Love makes the marriage and the family; Reason builds the house in which it can thrive. Love hears the music; Reason crafts the instrument upon which it can be played. Love imagines the art; Reason stretches the canvas and mixes the paints. Love engenders a vision for a new world; Reason builds it.

Love is not an ideology. It is a way of living, with faith and reason as its instruments in the world. Love demands that faith and reason be used as tools, not of cruelty or domination or exploitation or violence, but of justice, righteousness and peace; not as swords or spears, but as plowshares and pruning hooks.

The challenges to faith in our time are not challenges to living faith as much as they are to dead religion. The danger in these challenges is that they will shake our faith and our reason. Shall they make us ashamed to give thanks? Shall we become self-conscious about gathering to worship the Creator of Life? Shall we be embarrassed to pray for others? Shall we no longer use our faith to dream and our reason to labor toward the peaceable kingdom to come?

I think not. I think we will still keep to living faith while the irrational doctrines and dogmas of dead religion fall all around us. I think we will still forge our faith on the anvil of reason and throw it forward in memory of those who went before us and in hope for those who will follow.

REVELATION AND RAPTURE

First some background about the Book of Revelation: This is one of the hardest books of the Bible for people of a liberal theological persuasion to get their heads around. As a result, we gladly steer clear of it as often as possible. The fevered dream imagery of the author, John of Patmos also called St. John the Divine and John the Revelator, evokes angels, many-headed monsters, dragons, lakes of fire and snarling Satan himself.

Revelation has been the fountainhead of countless "end-of-the-world" cults and preachers through the ages right down to the wildly popular "Left Behind" series of novels describing the tribulations of the late 20th century and the so-called 'Rapture' about which I will have much more to say later.

If you fear the future and hate your enemies and are looking to save your own self-righteous carcass, this book of Revelation may be just the thing for you. Revelation is not your "Sweet, Gentle Jesus" sort of writing that we find in gospel accounts of the Sermon on the Mount, all filled with lilies of the field and birds of the air and little children and turning the other cheek and letting our little light shine. In the Book of Revelation, Jesus is a fierce and angry judge seated high on a heavenly throne separating the good from the wicked and consigning the wicked to a horrible destruction. It does not make for good bed-time reading for those who are less than totally convinced of their own impeccable goodness, or not sure about the utter wickedness of others.

The author, according to tradition, was the brother of James and the son of Zebedee. He was a fisherman, a disciple, and later an apostle. Modern scholars are not so sure of this authorship, but we do know that the author of Revelation was imprisoned by the Roman authorities and put to hard labor quarrying stone on the island of Patmos in the Aegean Sea during a time when Christians were being grievously persecuted far and wide.

Their crime was declaring that God was the supreme ruler and refusing to worship the man-made cult of the Roman emperors. John probably wrote during the reign of the emperor Domitian (A.D. 81-96) who did not go down in history as a benign and enlightened ruler. According to Roman historians Tacitus and Juvenal, Domitian's reign was so brutal that his own wife arranged for him to be butchered to put an end to it. It is hard to imagine the cruel conditions of imprisonment and punishment reserved for dissenters in those days.

In our own land and our own time when freedom of speech is accepted—though it clearly still needs to be tirelessly defended—we make jokes about the Christians and the lions. We even make jokes about crucifixion. But 2,000 years ago those who peacefully pursued their own faith and resisted the entrenched power of the Roman Empire suffered horribly by torture, imprisonment, and the abominably cruel execution of crucifixion which was inflicted upon not just Jesus himself but also Peter, Andrew and thousands of others. Those who resisted the power of the empire, even peacefully, were judged to be outlaws and terrorists and dealt with accordingly. Resistance to the emperor meant horrible suffering and martyrdom.

On the subject of martyrdom, let me wander for a moment.

We still talk about "martyrs" when someone gives his or her life to a selfless cause. But tragically the most frequent martyrdom today seems to be that of religious extremists who blow up themselves and those they hate in a horrendous bloodbath of destruction. In truth, these suicidal killers have been cruelly misled and are not martyrs at all. The true martyrs today and through the ages are those who are destroyed while harmlessly living out their lives and following their beliefs, like the hundreds of thousands of innocent Iraqis who have died in that devastated country while simply worshipping as they see fit, feeding their families, and going about their daily business. If there is a paradise for martyrs, justice dictates that it is innocents like these who will be welcomed there, not their murderers.

Back to our narrative: The historical reality of Christians bravely living out their faithful and peaceful lives in the face of the brutality of the Roman Empire goes a long way toward explaining the harsh and disturbing language of the Book of Revelation. New Testament scholar Martin Rist says: "In Revelation the criterion of righteous conduct is perfect loyalty to God and Christ, which is demonstrated by absolute refusal to worship the emperor or the state in any manner whatever, even though the death penalty might be invoked against the nonconformists." Given all this brutal history maybe we can begin to understand some of the colorful horrors of Revelation.

And yet, there is another vision even more challenging and compelling here in the Book of Revelation, rising like a phoenix from the ashes. It is the underlying vision of the reign, not of kings or rulers or emperors, but of justice and righteousness: the reign of God. It is the echo of Isaiah's peaceable kingdom. It is the ancient and holy dream from deep in the human heart. Look at the record.

In Isaiah (8th century B.C.) we read about the coming end of the world: "Behold, the Lord will lay waste the earth and make it desolate, and he will twist its surface and scatter its inhabitants.

And it shall be, as with the people, so with the priest; as with the slave, so with the master; as with the maid, so with her mistress... The earth shall be utterly laid waste and despoiled."

Then, in the very next chapter, redemption follows destruction as we read: "The Lord will make a feast for all peoples, a feast of fat things and wine... He will destroy the covering that is spread over all nations. He will swallow up death forever and wipe away tears from all faces."

Moving ahead to John the Revelator, chapter 6 (1st c. A.D.), we read, "I looked and behold there was a great earthquake and... the sky vanished like a scroll that is rolled up, and every mountain and hill was removed... The kings of the earth, the great men and the generals and the rich and the strong: everyone slave and free hid among the rocks..."

Then in the very next chapter redemption again follows destruction: "I looked and behold a great multitude from every nation, from all tribes and peoples and tongues standing before the throne of God... They shall hunger no more, neither thirst anymore... and God will wipe away every tear from their eyes."

It is phenomenal how little that dream changed in nearly a thousand years between Isaiah and John the Revelator. The same dream echoes almost 2000 years later in our own nation's history in the stirring words of Abraham Lincoln, and in the dream of Dr. Martin Luther King Jr. See how the dream of justice and righteousness will not die, no matter how the powers and principalities of this world try to kill it.

The truth of the matter is that this is not just the dream of Isaiah or Jesus or John the Revelator. It is not just the dream of ancients and moderns alike. It is God's eternal dream for the Creation. This vision rises up again and again in our tradition. It is woven through our historical memories. It rises up all over the world today from Alabama to Zimbabwe. And I am confident that we will discover one day that it is also embedded in the DNA of every cell in every body on the whole earth.

What does this timeless revelation mean to us today? Three preacher's points here.

First, this timeless revelation means that we cannot give our ultimate loyalty to any earthly emperor, prince, king, queen, celebrity, president, priest or ruler. We are to give our ultimate loyalty to God, to each other, and to the vision of justice, righteousness and peace.

Second, this ancient vision of the peaceable kingdom is not about politics. It cannot be forced upon any people by any other by any means. It is not about religion. It cannot come to pass by one religion converting all others.

And third, this vision does not mean that some will be saved and others lost. The vision of the peaceable kingdom is most decidedly not about personal salvation and everyone else be damned. This sort of 'salvation' is a snare and a delusion. No, worse: It is diabolical. And this is what bothers me so much about idolizing the Book of Revelation and the *Left Behind* phenomenon. Though I can forgive a starving, imprisoned first century John breaking stone in a quarry for judging others so harshly, it's harder to forgive a wealthy 20th century so-called 'Christian' novelist flying around in his private jet.

Here's what bothers me about the whole idea of individual salvation or damnation. Here's what bothers me about the 'Rapture.' For the life of me I can't see why any Christian would expect or even want a free pass out of the tribulations of this world to "meet the Lord in the air" leaving behind suffering family, friends and neighbors who had not been 'saved' by uttering a few magic words.

Jesus Christ himself was left behind. Jesus Christ himself never sought a free pass out of the tribulations of life on earth. He met suffering head on and did everything in his power to heal it and redeem it, to the last hour of his life, and to the last ounce of his strength.

The timeless dream of Isaiah, Jesus, John and so many others arises by itself in all times and all places. It brings redemption out of destruction. It will never be stopped or stayed. We are redeemed by redeeming others. We are relieved from suffering by relieving the suffering of others. We are healed by healing others. Our tears are wiped away when we wipe away the tears of others. And in that day when all the tears are wiped away, all nations and people will see their salvation together.

❋
Winter
❋

THE CHRISTMAS TREE

Though in latter years it has lost some of its magic, going out on a cold December day to bring home the Yuletide tree is a primal rite, usually falling to the males of the clan, stirring ancestral memories too deep for words, and repeated from Norman Rockwell calendars to whisky advertisements for so long that it is etched in the collective unconscious. We've been getting Christmas trees off our land in Pembroke for years, balsam firs that I mow around and trim up once a year. Oftentimes other family members go along, but this time I went alone. I took two trees, one for the house and one for the church. For all its deep drama and adventure, however, cutting your own trees in the wild may not make the most sense either economically or ecologically.

Here's why: In the course of this ceremonial quest, I paid almost $50 for gas at Johnson's Mobil Mart, bought my favorite cardiac breakfast (sausage, eggs and home fries) at the Waco Diner for $8 with a tip for the sad-eyed waitress, got two small coffees at the Irving mart at $1.50 each, plus a dollar for the matchless *Quoddy Tides* newspaper and 75 cents for the *Bangor Daily*. Then there was $592 for fuel oil to top off the tank at the house in Eastport, two days away from work, and 240 miles of wear and tear and depreciation at 25 cents a mile on the old truck for another $60.

With raised eyebrows any environmentalist would point out the huge production of unnecessary greenhouse gases in this foolish endeavor; and with tight lips any accountant would project a cost in real dollars of about $323 per tree. I plead guilty as charged. And yet, when I went down the slope past our camp on that morning, the air was cold and still and tiny frost feathers flocked everything with a sparkling radiance as the sun peeked over the tops of the trees. The tracks of mice and a large buck zigzagged around the clearing. When the first tree fell softly on the snow and the healing balsam odor exploded into the bitter air, a bald eagle dropped and soared silently out over the bay from the huge spruce on the shore about 100 feet away. Dragging the trees one at a time about a quarter mile through the deep, crunching snow to where my truck was parked on the town road, my heart pounded hot blood into my chilly limbs and hammered at the crust of modern corrosion and hostility between us and Creation until it all fell away leaving a shining primal man dragging his quarry home: Not a moose or a buck as a boon for the bodies of loved ones, but balsam fir as a balm for their souls.

The environmentalist and the economist might rightly waggle their fingers and declare that the two fir trees were far too expensive. But I say they were free. And so was I: as free as I have ever been. Coming home on Route 1 in Machias, amidst thousands of square miles of fir trees on every side, I saw a big sign at Pinkham Lumber that read "ON SALE! Artificial Xmas Trees $19.99."

Not this year, by the old bones of Odin; not this year.

CHRISTMAS

The balsam fir *Abies balsamea* is central to the celebration of Christmas around here. Beginning in early November after a couple of hard frosts, tree farmers start cutting their trees to be shipped off to the cities and tippers go out into the forests to cut balsam brush for wreathes, swags, and other seasonal decorations. I usually cut some wild trees at our camp on Cobscook Bay: an eight-footer for the house, an eighteen-footer for the church, and some smaller ones for friends or just for greens. Sometimes their branches are decorated with tassels of Old Man's Beard, a pale green lichen, or even a thrush or white-throat's nest. Fresh-cut balsam has the most alluring fragrance imaginable. With one whiff it can transport you back through the years or far out into the woods. To open the door into the cold, old dining room where we stand the tree is to step into a fairy-tale. The balmy aroma, the lights, the clunky old handmade ornaments, the snow seen out the windows, the memories are overwhelming. They take an ancient Middle Eastern desert legend and transform it into a living, singing saga of the boreal forests. In the twinkling of an eye they translate this beloved tale from Aramaic to Algonkian and wrap us warmly in its enchantments.

Around here the spirits of the towns are mostly Christian. But the spirits of the forests are Algonquin; the spirits of the snow and ice are Inuit; the spirits of the mountains are Buddhist; the spirits of the big trees, rocks and waterfalls are Shinto; the spirits of the animals are Neolithic; and the spirits of the bays and islands are Celtic, Druid and Pagan. If you stay in town, Christianity might be all you need. But, if you wander far out beyond the towns, Christianity may not be enough.

One of the great benefits of living way out on the narrow two-lane roads far from the Interstate, far from the cities, and face to face with the forces of the Creation, is that you can walk directly out into the presence of the Great Benevolent Spirit which created the entire world—yourself included—out of all the same stuff. The fundamentalist devotees of any religion will insist that their scriptures and traditions are the only true ones and that all others are false. They will insist that they have the whole answer, and unless you believe as they do, you are doomed. But around here, it's nearly impossible to make that case, as much as some still try.

To see the limits of the orthodox view, just walk outside. See the round wreathes of balsam fir carefully constructed in the fertile female shape of the circle, as they have been for thousands of years. See the fir trees set up in so many homes, the ageless emblem of male power. These are symbols of the Old Faith, far older than any organized religion.

See the tracks of the smaller creatures in the snow writing their truth in a strange, runic scripture that can be read, yes, but only by the fearless. Feel the cold wind from the frozen North, or the drear, wet wind from the East off the Great Water. Hear the last geese high above honking and beating their way South. See the lights in the windows of the white houses and the white churches with their long spires reaching heavenward topped by weather-vanes pointing to the four directions. See the sun start its sojourn back up toward the peak of the heavens and feel the gut-deep joy at the returning of the light. Hold a new baby in its little snowsuit, hat and mittens, and know something no theology can teach. Know that here no one religion can ever contain or explain the truth of this overwhelming Creation: present, past, nor future. Know that the true believer and the fundamentalist hide out in fear of the real, wild world, dripping, dying, breathing, bleeding, melting, freezing, birthing, and healing; wholly created, wholly free, wholly original, wholly authentic... Wholly Holy.

Hanukkah, Christmas, Yule, Solstice, Kwanzaa, Rohatsu—they are all beautiful but ever so pale imitations of the authentic, original faith of heaven and earth. Please, fear not to open wide your heart at this luminous season. Fear not the warmongers, the terrorists, the life-haters, the bombers, the diabolical conspirators, the fiendish fiscal controllers. Fear not those you love. Fear not those you do not love. Fear not, for they have no final power over you.

Fear not, for now while the bear sleeps and the porcupine slumbers, they, the geese, the herons, the ospreys count the days until they can come back to life here. Fear not, for now the light is returning, a Holy Child is coming to birth, bringing glad tidings of great joy that will be to the whole Creation.

When we look at the Nativity alongside other holidays we see it is strikingly different. Halloween celebrates the dead. Veterans Day is a celebration of those who fought in wars. Pearl Harbor Day marks our entry into the Second World War. Presidents Day honors Washington who led our country in the Revolutionary War, and Lincoln who led our country in the Civil War. Then we have Memorial Day remembering those who died in all our wars. Then we have July 4th honoring the men who signed the Declaration of Independence, which was also a declaration of war. These are our major holidays when we close the post office and schools and march in parades, celebrating what? Mighty men, wars, and death.

Now, along comes Christmas turning the world of heroes and wars and death upside down. Here's Christmas celebrating the birthday of a weak, helpless baby, born in poverty of an unwed mother, virtually homeless. He never owned a home, never left his own country, never wrote a book, never led an army or even fought in a war, never ruled a nation. Yet, who in human history has changed more hearts and inspired more compassion and love for children, the weak and the helpless? Who is more loved and admired by all ages? Who was a braver preacher of peace on earth and justice for all than this Jesus whose birth we remember at Christmas?

Most of us start out just like the child who wrote our Advent poem last Sunday. "I'll give my life to the light, to the warmth, to Peace, to the World," he wrote. But when we grow up we often lose that light and vision of peace. "Shades of the prison house" begin to close around us. We gradually change and harden and begin to accept the suffering of the poor and helpless. We say, "They are not like us, they are ignorant, they have bad habits, they hate to work." We start to accept the cruelties of war saying, "Sure, we all want peace, but we have to be realistic. We have to have wars to 'make the world safe for democracy'... or 'to destroy the evil ones'... or 'to bring peace.'"

When we grow up and acquire a certain amount of power and responsibility in this world, it is easy to get an inflated idea of our own importance, like the ancient priest who prayed so many times as the sun rose that he began to believe that the sun rose because he was praying. It is like the manager of a business who thinks that unless he works harder and harder, the business will fail. It is like the minister who thinks that unless every sermon he preaches is better than the last, the church will fail, or the mother or father who fears that unless they do more and more and more for the family, they will fail.

Likewise, we may get to thinking that it is by our efforts that Christmas happens. We have to get the tree up, the lights strung, the ornaments hung, the cards sent out, the presents bought and the services of worship orchestrated and performed.

It is our illusion that it is up to us to see that the world turns, the seasons progress, the creatures give birth, and life goes on. It is our illusion that we are in charge, not Almighty God. Elizabeth and Mary did not have this illusion. Did Mary say, "I have done great things for God'? No. She said, "God has done great things for me." She knew where the power is.

Going up onto the mountain at this time of the year one sees that great prominence resting, as though asleep. The woods are hushed and still. The birds of summer are gone. So are the people, for the most part. The squirrels, porcupines and foxes are denned-up and less active. The trees are dormant. Nothing is being born, nothing is growing. At this time of the year, I imagine that the mountain is completely and utterly in the hands of the Creator, leaving God in charge; quietly, joyfully, ecstatically trusting God. Upon her body, the mountain bears the truth which we struggle to find in our worship, our prayers, our theologies. We bear the same truth in our own bodies, as did Elizabeth and Mary.

Somewhere up there on the mountain is a black bear, *Ursus Americanus,* sleeping as only bears can sleep. She spent the fall foraging far and wide for acorns, beechnuts, field mice, apples, insects, roots, and carrion. For months now she will eat nothing, drink nothing and remain completely at rest, as though she were dead. But she is not dead. In deep midwinter, the coldest time of the year, she will give birth. Her two or three cubs will wait, too, suckling quietly in her warm embrace until Spring. While we are rushing around down here trying to get our shopping done during one of the most hectic times of our year, she is up there dreaming and meditating and purring her own *Magnificat* in her den under the hem of Heaven and waiting upon the Lord to renew her strength, and raise her up with her young.

There is something very holy about this; like a liturgy being performed on the tiniest and grandest scale at once, and every-thing in between, yet almost invisible to us in our small, cramped daily lives. So, pause for a moment. Look inward and imagine that our bodies are small sanctuaries and that the cells in our bodies are worshippers singing praises to the Creator. Then, lift the roof and look outward. Imagine that the whole universe is a vast cathedral, billions of light-years in every direction, filled with the ancient and majestic music of the spheres, and that all the creatures, planets, stars, and galaxies being born, living, dying and being born again are the worshippers and the celebrants. And then consider, if you can, that this is not simply your imagination, but the truth.

Elizabeth knew this truth when she said, "We are blessed." Mary knew this when she said, "God has done wonderful things, lifting up the lowliest." Within our own bodies and the bodies of all living things from the greatest to the least, within each egg, sperm, seed, spore, bud, cone, nut and root; a holy birth is coming. This is a universe not only of God the Father, but also of God the Mother, God the Son, God the Daughter, and God the Midwife. Everything, every single particle of the cosmos becomes a part of the Great Ceremony of conception, birth, life, death, and rebirth.

And then, in that moment, the whole Creation becomes the holy Mother of Christmas.

DR. KING'S BIRTHDAY

After Christmas and New Year's we take down the greens and the decorations and look ahead to cold months when the ground is white, and most of the people are too. The Martin Luther King holiday comes at just the right time, firing us up with righteous memories among the older and fervent hopes among the younger. We comb the hymnal for "spirituals" and sing them with all the soul we can muster. We clap awkwardly during the singing and even say the occasional "A-men" before sliding back into our comfortable Yankee solemnity. But we're a good deal warmer and more convinced when we leave than when we came in.

We honor Dr. Martin Luther King Jr., as one of the greatest voices for justice and peace this nation has ever heard, and certainly the greatest preacher of the century, if not the millennium. By 1964, Dr. King had become a leader in the global struggle for human rights, an eloquent critic of the Vietnam War and a stirring spokesman for world peace.

This morning we'll hear the words of the Old Testament prophets along with Dr. King's powerful oratory framed by the poor words of a small-town preacher who, without apology, considers Dr. King to be a prophet equal to the prophets of old, holding to the same standards they did in calling judgment upon a great nation. God is righteous and just, and we all bear the burden of that judgment, but the powerful today, as in former times, carry the greatest burden.

In a time when the United States is without dispute the most powerful nation the world has ever seen, while the world emulates our culture, while American English is on the tongues of nearly every nation, and while millions are seeking a home upon our shores, it is a tragedy of Biblical proportions that instead of being purveyors of peace and teachers of liberty, we have become dealers of weapons and promoters of violence.

It is the height of irony that the United States threatens to use weapons of mass destruction against those who follow our example in building weapons of mass destruction. It is the epitome of hypocrisy to lash out at other nations for pursuing technologies of violence which the United States created and sold or even gave to them. We turn to the prophet Micah, eighth century B.C.:

"And (God) shall judge among many people, and rebuke strong nations afar off; and they shall beat their swords into plowshares, and their spears into pruning hooks, nation shall not lift up sword against nation, neither shall they learn war anymore."

How can the United States expect other nations to lay down their arms when we are increasing our arsenal of weapons at a demonic rate? How can we demand that others submit to international law when we do not, nor wait for the direction of the United Nations before violently punishing other nations, nor submit to the judgments of the World Court when they go against us? Hear the prophet Amos:

"I despise your feast days (says the Lord)... Take from me the noise of thy songs, for I will not hear the melody... But let justice run down as waters, and righteousness as a mighty stream..."

Has the once tiny, courageous and struggling nation, which

fought to free itself from that great world bully George III, forgotten its insurgent origins? Have we forgotten that the revolution which gave birth to our nation had as its rallying cry, "We hold these truths to be self-evident that all men are created equal and endowed by their Creator with certain inalienable rights"? We turn to Dr. King:

"A true revolution of values will lay hands on the world order and say of war: "This way of settling differences is not just.' This business of burning human beings..., of filling... homes with widows and orphans, of injecting poisonous drugs of hate into the veins of people normally humane, of sending men home from dark and bloody battlefields physically handicapped and psychologically deranged, cannot be reconciled with wisdom, justice and love. A nation that continues year after year to spend more money on military defense than on programs of social uplift is approaching spiritual death."

The United States of America may be the mightiest country in this world, but we are not the greatest power. No. There is a far, far greater power whom we cannot buy with all of our money, persuade with all of our powers of persuasion, entertain with all our entertainment, or destroy with all of our weapons. There is a power that judges us today, a power that has judged every nation before us, a power that has brought so many great empires down. Dr. King again.

"Over the bleached bones and jumbled residues of numerous civilizations are written the pathetic words: 'Too late.' We still have a choice today: nonviolent coexistence or violent coannihilation. This may well be mankind's last chance to choose between chaos and community."

We are community people, small-town people trying to be good. It is easy to feel helpless as the morning paper and the evening news spread out before us pictures of a violent world. It is not that we do not feel. We look at the world and weep, or cry out in pity, remorse, and rage. We see the condition of even

Jerusalem, whose name means "city of peace," yet it too is torn by violence, and we hear the words of Jesus:

"And when he was come near, he beheld the city, and wept over it, saying, 'If thou hadst known... the things which make for peace! But now they are hid from thine eyes.'"

In the face of such wrong, it is tempting to content ourselves with going about our business in this most peaceful of places while the world is in turmoil, concluding that their is nothing we can do, tucked away as we are in little villages on the coast of Maine. But, there is plenty we can do. All it takes is conviction. Dr. King speaks again:

"I have the audacity to believe that people everywhere can have three meals a day for their bodies, education and culture for their minds, and dignity, equality and freedom for their spirits. I believe that what self-centered men have torn down, other-centered men can build up."

We can speak too, to make sure everyone on our peninsula has three square meals a day, no one is cold, our schools are the best they can be, to make the international trade in weapons of war a crime while lifting sanctions and embargoes on food and medicines to every country.

The heart of Dr. King's belief is the same as ours, the same dream of peace as dreamed by the Hebrew slaves in Egypt, by the prophets, by Jesus Christ, by African slaves locked in the holds of slave ships. It is God's dream *for* us that God dreams *with* us, even in the deepest dark of our fear and remorse. That dream will ever spring up to bring light into the darkness.

We are not alone in our crying from frustration and fear for the future. We weep and wail with the ages. The chorus of weeping swells to the heavens from Adam and Eve whose son slew his brother, from Pharaoh's slaves, from the prophets, from Jesus, from widows and orphans of wars, from Iraq, Afghanistan and Africa, Pakistan and India, Iran and Iraq, and from the streets of Oakland, Jerusalem and Gaza City, from political prisoners, and from small-town people trying to be good.

The tears of the ages flow together in a living, rolling current joining into mighty rivers of justice and ever-flowing streams of righteousness. These are our tears. These are Christ's tears. These are God's tears. We cry them out because we all have a dream—a dream shared by the ages, a dream that will never be stopped nor stayed.

These tears of pain come pouring forth to rust and corrode the weapons of war, and to water the seeds of hope, the seeds of peace, the tree of life whose fruit is for the healing of the nations. These tears of broken-ness and grief flow into an ocean of healing and a rising tide of hope which has today lifted an African-American family into the White House, and we pray, will wash every shore in days to come. Hear Dr. King one more time:

"I still believe that one day humanity will bow before the altars of God and be crowned triumphant over war and blood-shed—and non-violent redemptive good will shall proclaim the rule of the land. And the lion and the lamb shall lie down together and every one shall sit under vine and fig tree, and none shall be afraid. I still believe that we shall overcome."

ANNUAL MEETING

*

Nearly as important an observance as Christmas or Easter for Congregationalists is Annual Meeting Sunday. Here, this has been held in late January for longer than anyone can remember. Last January was our 240th. It gives us something to take our minds off the bleak midwinter landscape which stretches nearly unrelieved between the other two major holidays. Unfortunately, meeting in midwinter makes it most difficult for our summer people to attend as they are spending the season in comfortably warmer climes. So we simply have to struggle along without them with the assurance that we will hear from them when they return.

At a typical annual meeting, after worship, chowder, and the opening prayer, the minister will paint a sublime picture of the life and good works of the congregation over the past year and offer glowing predictions of the next so as to burnish his or her own reputation or simply buck up flagging self-esteem. Then, the treasurer will offer a far sterner scenario with hints of Divine Judgment on what will surely happen if we neglect our pledges to the church, or exceed our budget allotments or, worst of all, forget to turn in receipts for any purchases, such as paper cups.

(We outlawed Styrofoam years ago.)

Occasionally there will be a controversial matter brought to the floor. One I remember well was whether to purchase an entirely new hymnal or continue to use the old standard. As might be expected, the Modernists and the Traditionalists quickly divided themselves into opposing parties and waded into the fray with great vigor and surprising stamina, especially for the Traditionalists who were mostly well past middle age. In typical fashion after a relatively sanguine interchange we voted to keep both hymnals. Now we enjoy a much richer worship experience while tripping good-naturedly over all those hymnals and muttering under our breath. Discussions over same-sex marriages were not always so cordial, but we managed to resolve that issue too, after only about ten years.

I have included part of an annual meeting sermon in this entry, but far more important is the fish chowder and cornbread dinner that precedes the meeting as it has for uncounted generations. Below are the necessary recipes to serve 50 eager congregants.

Kickshaw Fish Chowder
½ lb. butter
3 lbs. yellow onions
10 14 ½ oz cans diced potatoes
½ cup Old Bay seasoning (sine qua non)
10 lbs haddock
6 to 12 12 oz. cans evaporated milk

Saute onions in butter till translucent. (You can imagine what the aroma of onions sautéing downstairs does to concentration during the sermon.) Add potatoes, seasoning and water to cover. Simmer 10 minutes. Layer fish on top, cover, and poach for 10 minutes. Stir in canned milk and keep warm an hour or more. Full flavor develops upon standing.

Corn Bread
7 ½ cups white flour
4 ½ cups yellow corn meal
2 cups sugar
4 tablespoons baking powder (NOT baking soda)
2 teaspoons salt
6 cups skim milk
1 ½ cups oil
6 eggs

Preheat ovens to 400. Beat wet, add to dry, bake in greased 8 x 8 pans 20-25 minutes. Put in ovens during Offertory to serve hot right after service.

"Now, I ask you, brothers and sisters, for the sake of Jesus Christ, that you all speak the same thing, and that there be no divisions among you; but that you be perfectly joined together in the same mind and in the same judgment. For I have been told... that there are dissensions among you... Is Christ divided?"

It seems unbelievable that the venerable elders of the church who over the centuries composed the common lectionary from which we draw today's scriptures could have known how many New England Congregational churches would hold their annual meetings on this particular Sunday, as we are. Nevertheless, the traditional selections are uncannily appropriate.

In the gospel, we hear Jesus calling for repentance for heaven is at hand. Maine songwriter David Mallet, whom Becky and I love, has a song called *Closer to Truth* in which he sings, "In dangerous times, we are closer to truth, we are nearer to God, when our lives are on the line, we are nearer to God..." David Mallett sings about the death of a friend; and any of us who have attended a death or had a brush with death ourselves, any of us who have been present at the moment of birth, any of us who have had cancer or a close friend with cancer know this. God is near, heaven is at hand in dangerous times.

Peter Gomes, in his matchless commentary on the Bible titled *The Good Book*, says that at these times we are in what the Irish call "the thin places" where the distance between us and God is so slight as to be almost transparent, and the illumination of the divine is keenly felt, bathing with a muted light even those who have been living in darkness. We have seen it so many times.

This is not to suggest that the simple, mundane event of a congregational meeting is a brush with death—though in some churches at some times it is darned close. Rather, it is suggesting that the cosmic Christ is present at our worship and our meetings, and that here we are in the presence of all who came before us. Most of us have felt the presence of, say, Jonathan Fisher when we gather. But in some sense, all of those who have given their full measure of devotion to this church and then gone to be with God are here too. This church today is not simply us and our hopes, dreams, and annoyances. It is also them. Jesus is here. So are Jonathan and Dolly Fisher. So are so many of our number who have gone before. When we speak the name of God or Jesus, past, present and future, earth and heaven are collapsed into the present thin place. Heaven is at hand.

Do we think that the kind of love that Jesus showed by laying down his life for everyone who would come after him was stopped from crossing the oceans of distance or the centuries of time? No. Do we think that the prayers our predecessors earnestly uttered in this hall have evaporated into nothing? No. That love and those prayers are alive in this place now. Time and distance have no power over love. Do we think that the spirits of those who were baptized here, married here, and mourned here have fled forever, leaving no caring behind? We don't. Heaven is at hand.

In this eternal and timeless context, it is right and good that we repent of our little sins, aggressions and quarrels, and turn ourselves over to the larger body, which extends backward and forward in time and distance from here to Jerusalem and back all the way around the world. Let me hasten to add that when we say that we are part of a larger holy body that is not to say that we are better. We are not God's chosen people. God chose all people. But not all people choose God. When we do, we set a high standard for ourselves. We open ourselves up to even greater judgment.

Our predecessors put their faith in the radically democratic congregational meeting. They were punished and oppressed for insisting on the truth of their own prayerful reading of scripture and their own self-determination in religion. Some were hanged, burned, imprisoned. They may have disagreed among themselves from time to time. They may have had their dissensions and divisions, but it is safe to suggest that from where they are now, they're hoping that we will be perfectly joined together in this thing that's bigger than all of us.

The congregational meeting, for which our ancestors struggled, was the model for town meeting. It is a present council of those who gathered here in the past, who are gathered here today, and who will be here when we are all gone to dust. At its best, it is a gem of spiritual ecology and direct democracy. At its worst, it ranks somewhere beneath a dog fight. With that in mind, I offer this *Primer for Congregational Meetings*:

- For congregational churches, the will of the meeting, informed by prayer, is as close to the will of the Holy Spirit as we can practically expect to get; therefore, it is wise to begin meetings with heart-felt prayer and end with a benediction or hymn. These, however, should not be considered a substitute for lightning rods on the steeple when Heaven is so close at hand.
- The purpose of church meetings is similar to the sea chantey or work song, that is, to do the work at hand as effectively as possible, and to allow every voice to be heard while the work is

being done. For the first purpose, it is critical that an impartial chair or moderator be appointed, that an agenda be prepared, and that standards of procedure such as Robert's Rules of Order be followed as carefully as the ship's captain follows chart and compass. If the meeting loses sight of its objective and is allowed to wander off course, it is likely to get lost and go upon the rocks with injury to crew and damage to property and investors. For the second purpose, it is important that the chair or moderator put the voice of the whole body of the meeting foremost, and prevent the timidity of some from being drowned out by the temerity of others. Some may try to dominate the meeting and should be promptly, but gently, thwarted. A good moderator will call on members in the order in which they have raised their hands, and may even ask for the opinions of the silent, if for no other reason than to verify that they are still among the living.

- Speakers should be brief, remembering that a four-minute speech—or four one-minute speeches—to a meeting of 50 people will rob a full three hours and twenty minutes of precious collective lifetime from the fleeting sojourn their brothers and sisters are provided upon this blessed earth.

- Socializing is not the primary purpose of church meetings but is a great incidental benefit. A good plan will allow for socializing both before and after, but not during the meeting.

- Leave them laughing. The Bible may not be particularly funny, but anyone who has lived for more than three or four decades knows that God has a wry sense of humor. Perhaps that is why a wise Providence has given us the congregational church meeting. Here humor is the truest leaven. It is far better to leave with the sweet taste of laughter and love in your mouth than with the bile of anger or the acid of self-righteousness.

ANGER

I noticed as I approached age 60 that, in a conflict situation, I would sometimes jump over my usual responses of understanding, compassion, humor, problem-solving, forgiveness or patience, and began to go directly to resentment, crankiness and anger. This worried me because it has not usually been my style, and I have hated it in too many men my age and older (and younger for that matter). I decided I'd best study the matter before I became an angry old man too. "Old" and "Man," I can't do anything about, but I can do something about "Angry."

To "unpack" this, as the professors say, let's look at gender. I don't want to inflame the politically correct, or incorrect, so I will speak from experience instead of ideology. It seems to be mostly *men* who are angry. Men have long been used to treating one man as the big boss, the king, the 'alpha male,' while the other men fall in line behind or below in the ancient hierarchical social system.

In this primal system, young bucks challenge the alpha male who always has to be ready to defend himself and quash any sign of rebellion or usurpation. This is very stressful for males, and anger is a ready response to stress. On the other hand, many women seem to be more comfortable with a cooperative and deliberative process in which everyone is heard and accommodated and no one has to be the big boss all the time.

Next, why is it old men? In the church, I have been on the receiving end of the anger of old men more times then I care to count. I call this "Retired Executive Syndrome." An older man, who has had an important position in business, medicine, law, teaching, the church or other white-collar institutions, retires; or perhaps we should say, is retired. He moves to Blue Hill and joins the church. Shortly, he realizes that his sphere of influence has been severely diminished. He feels diminished himself, for several reasons:

First, because he was retired when he may have had a lot of energy and experience to offer and his retirement happened simply because he was too old. Next, things have changed at home. His wife is now getting, as the old saying goes, "twice the husband and half the paycheck." He has been changed overnight from a Big Cheese to a Honeydew: "Honey, do this. Honey, do that."

Third, he sees the church doing things in a way never tolerated in his previous profession (even though this church has survived nicely for almost 240 years, far longer than the company he used to work for.) And, fourth, he sees a man younger than himself who seems to be the "boss" of the church, but is a pitiful and wretched example of a president or CEO. The retired executive rolls up his sleeves and wades into the holy fray, bringing an unholy load of frustration and anger.

Some examples: A highly-placed editor at a large publishing house is retired and volunteers to edit the church newsletter—a sure recipe for disaster. Waving a copy of the latest newsletter, he storms into the office of the church secretary who produces the newsletter, and berates her for typographical errors, improper margins, lay-out, grammar and so forth, leaving the overworked and underpaid church secretary in a state of near hysteria.

A retired executive from a large, multi-national corporation becomes chair of the church's Trustees and begins attacking the Outreach budget for wasting money on indigent people and politically-suspect causes. A financial director retired from a business or institution decides to start an aggressive new stewardship effort to get those deadwood, non-giving members off the rolls and get ever more money from the giving members. A retired minister becomes enraged by what he perceives as a pastoral error by his younger colleague. An older newspaper editor walks out of church and writes scathing editorials about politics from the pulpit.

Retired Executive Syndrome is serious. Some of these men are able to adjust, downsize and redirect their ambitions and energies into serving the life of an ancient small town and church. But some are not. They become more angry and pull away, sometimes leaving wreckage in their wake. Or, they die from a heart attack, stroke, or cancer. I have seen these sad results many times.

To move from our small-town stage to a world stage, why do we find so many angry old men in powerful positions in government? Why do so many of our elected leaders seem so stern, rigid and humorless, so bent on punishing, so intent on frightening others or strutting about in military gear? Why are they so inclined to behaviors that would not be tolerated in any kindergarten or elementary school in the country? Why do they always want to have the all the weapons and all the answers, even when their weapons are a threat to the whole world and their answers are repeatedly proven to be wrong? Why are so many of our angry male leaders unable to dance and sing for us, or love us and inspire us, and make us feel good and generous and hopeful, instead of bad and selfish and fearful? Why are they so serious and scary all the time?

I would suggest that these angry old men are so serious and scary all the time because they are seriously scared, like our retired executives, because they know their sphere of influence is diminishing and, in the way the world is working, they are sooner or later going to be retired against their will. They fear that the inherited, hierarchical, punishing alpha-male model which they bought into, at the price of deeply compromising their own compassion, is losing its grip on the world; and they are feeling that they bought into an obsolete model, at great cost to themselves. They bought a Hummer and Honda is putting them out of business.

The model of the weak serving the powerful to which these men sold themselves has been tried—and is still being tried—but it has failed to make the world a better and more peaceful place time and again over the last 3,000 years. It is failing now because it is an evolutionary dead-end. Someone said that a fanatic is one who, when discovering his efforts do not achieve his goals, redoubles his efforts instead of changing his goals.

The world wants to move on, and will move on, and it will leave the angry old men behind. That's why they are seriously scared. That's why they are angry. And that's why they are very dangerous right now. The old order is slowly changing, making way for the new. I know how slowly change comes in a church of 100 or 200 members. This makes me more patient about the slow pace of change in a world of nearly 5 billion members.

The old myth of Nature "red in tooth and claw" has been used by angry males as a defense of wars waged by other angry males, as though such mass brutality is a universal natural phenomenon. In reality, war—defined as the mass killing of one's own species—is largely limited to male humans. Some social insects engage in the mass killing of similar, but rarely identical species, but most often only in the wake of the disruption of their environment by human interference, according to E.O. Wilson, probably the greatest authority on social insects.

Further, there is logical proof that the uncontrolled alpha-male model, regardless of what value it may have had in the past, is an evolutionary dead end for the human race because the angry alpha-male, if uncontrolled, will eventually destroy himself.

Here is the proof. First, he will destroy his male rivals. Then, he will destroy any mates or offspring who challenge his authority. Finally, he is left alone to die with no help, comfort, or support. In Nature, any male is controlled by his food supply, which is in turn controlled by weather and fertility and other factors beyond his control. He is controlled by diseases he cannot cure. He is controlled by his own aging and death. These are natural limits on the power of any creature. No angry old male can rule the world, or even his own house, if his mate is awake and empowered.

What's an angry old male to do, then? His first job is to rule himself; to rule over his anger, his violence, his greed, his selfishness, his lust for conquest. His job is to bring his base passions under the rule of, not just his head, but his heart, mind and soul, so they can serve the world. Any man whose heart cannot control his own lowest instincts will be an unsuccessful leader of others. Many powerful men have chosen the controlling of others over the far more difficult task of controlling themselves.

This has brought the world to a near-perpetual state of war. In the last century we have seen a war to make the world safe for democracy, a war against fascism, a cold war, wars on communism, hundreds of territorial and ethnic wars, a war on drugs, a war on cancer, and now we are told that we are in a war on terrorism that may never end. And, terrorism—the killing of innocent civilian non-combatants to gain political goals—has not diminished.

To the contrary, since the demented "war on terrorism" began, terrorism has increased. In a nihilistic orgy, angry men are blowing themselves up all over the world in a blind rage to kill innocent civilians—the elderly, women and children—for some twisted fantasy of male power or heaven or, God help us, world peace.

Millions of soldiers and innocent civilians have died in military wars engaged during the last century, more than in any similar period in history. None of these wars has finally accomplished its stated goals. The world is not safe for democracy, or free of fascism or communism or terrorism. In the context of the Iraq war, senior UN envoy Lakhdar Brahimi insisted that, "there is never a military solution to any problem."

The war model has consistently failed in other contexts, as well. The war on drugs has failed; illegal drug trade is burgeoning. The war on cancer has failed; cancer is claiming as many victims as ever.

No stronger proof than this can be found for the simple truth that, for all the horrible, fanatical battles over the ages, the one battle that needs so desperately to be won is within the hearts of angry men. Men, not women, are clearly the authors of war.

Now, I want to speak to angry old men, one of which I am in danger of becoming, and to women who have the greatest power over angry men. If you do not want to be an angry old man, here are some things you can do. And if you are a woman who does not want to live with an angry man, here's what you can urge to him:

Do not empower those who are more powerful than you; empower those who are less powerful.

Never employ anger, force or violence because there is no other choice; there are always other choices. Continually question and review your actions.

Defend yourself by not defending yourself. Use your influence by not using your influence.

If you have done wrong, say so. Seek forgiveness. Eat a little crow. It may be the healthiest meal you've had in a long time.

Learn and love music and art. They are other whole languages that will allow you to express your emotions without hurting, and with compassion.

Make nice things with your hands and give them away.

Learn to do nothing sometimes. Be silent. Let the voices in your head keep talking, but don't listen to or act on them.

Help others. Repair what is broken. Put out fires. Break up fights.

Speak by not speaking. Listen. Wait.

And most important: Walk, walk, walk. Walk off the anger, the fear, the guilt, the pain, and the despair at the world.

Walk until all is well.

FORGIVING

Forgiveness is not easy. We would like to have forgiveness without repentance, because if we forgive others without acknowledging what we have done wrong, it gives us an advantage over them. We say it every Sunday: "Forgive us our trespasses *as we forgive those who trespass against us."* Our forgiveness of others is empty without our own repentance, because it is our own failures that give us compassion for the failures of others.

Forgiving others can't happen without forgiving ourselves. Judas was unable to forgive himself or to receive the forgiveness of Jesus. Judas, unable to accept that free, graceful divine/human forgiveness, took his own life out of remorse. If we cannot forgive ourselves and accept God's forgiveness of us, we are lost. We can't pass forgiveness on to others, because we don't have any to pass on.

We've all heard, "Forgive and forget," but forgiving may mean not forgetting, it may mean remembering, and still forgiving. Hardest to forgive is the wrong done to us without remorse by those who seek no forgiveness. Yet, if we cannot forgive those who have done us wrong and not asked forgiveness, we remain their victims. Until we leave that wrong behind, it may be visited upon us again and again. It's so heartbreaking to hear about the death of Judas who could not accept forgiveness. It's so disturbing to hear about the angry families of murder victims who hover around the execution chamber of the murderer demanding "closure." Without forgiveness, there is no closure. The hurt goes on and on and on.

We hear Divine forgiveness in Christ's words from the cross, "Father, forgive them for they know not what they do." Of course, he was Jesus Christ, and we are not. But there are countless examples of Christ-like forgiveness by mere mortals like us. Beulah Mae Donald's son was lynched by Ku Klux Klansmen who were convicted in court with legal aid from the Southern Poverty Law Center. After the trial, Mrs. Donald was asked if she could ever forgive those responsible for her son's brutal murder. "I have already forgiven them," she said.

In South Africa, the hard work of the Truth and Reconciliation Commission, based on Christian standards of repentance and forgiveness and guided by Anglican Archbishop Desmond Tutu, allowed a country torn by the horrendous abuses of apartheid to be liberated from the past and begin healing into the future. Repentance and forgiveness are the Emmaus walk to freedom.

I'll leave the last word on forgiveness to the family of Allison Small from Vinalhaven, Maine, murdered by her lover who was convicted and sentenced to 40 years in prison. After the verdict, Allison Small's husband Fred Small said, "It's just. I don't hold any animosity." Allison Small's parents said, "If you don't forgive people, you yourself cannot be forgiven. We're all brothers and sisters... Who are we to judge? We're going to put flowers on Allison's grave and go home."

Repentance, then forgiveness; that is the walk. Was Judas forgiven? He was. Can we all be forgiven our trespasses? We can. How much? No less than we can forgive those who have trespassed against us.

ST. PATRICK'S DAY

*

By mid-March coastal Maine has a decidedly Irish cast to it. We may see some green for the first time in months and the weather is damp and foggy, veiling the mountain and the bay in a Celtic mist. Potted paper-white narcissus blooms fragrantly, garden seedlings rise greenly on window sills, and the florists put out the tulips and shamrocks. We dream at night of Spring; but still wake to Winter.

The subject is St. Patrick and the early Celtic Christian Church. I hasten to say that there is ample disagreement about many aspects of St. Patrick's life, but not about all of it. As with much of Western history between the sack of Rome in 410 AD and the coronation of Charlemagne in 800, documentation is slight and legend is abundant. But, most sources would agree upon the outline I will here present of Patrick's remarkable life. If you want to dig deeper, you might read *Celtic Christianity, Ecology and Holiness* by Christopher Bamford and *How the Irish Saved Civilization* by Thomas Cahill. Or just listen to the fiddle music of Kevin Burke or Natalie McMaster.

The Saint Patrick of legend was a powerful wizard known for driving the snakes (and the Druids) out of Ireland by the power of his magic. The Patrick of history was all that and more. It's true that there were no snakes in Ireland after Patrick, but there were none before him either. Born around 397 AD, or 386, or earlier, or later, in Scotland or Wales, but definitely not in Ireland, Patrick became a monumental figure in the history of the British Isles, a charismatic and progressive leader, and a remarkable poet.

At the age of 15, Patrick was abducted from his home and taken into slavery in Ireland. He spent years as a shepherd alone on the barren moors. During this time his body grew from a boy's to a man's and his spirit did the same. Like another shepherd, David, Patrick heard the voice of his Creator in the barren lands and became an inspired poet.

After making his way home, Patrick dedicated himself to the Christian faith. He received a minimal formal church education in Gaul, now France. According to Cahill, Patrick's Latin was eccentric at best and must be translated with a good measure of imagination. Yet, many of Patrick's words have survived to this day including the famous "Breastplate" which appears in countless collections and even in the Book of Common Prayer. The "Breastplate" is part of "The Deer's Cry" which identifies the Christian God with the Creator of the whole universe. And though he didn't give an inch to the Druids, Patrick included a version of the ancient prayer to the four directions so common in nature-centered religions like the Druids', and emphasizes the Trinity because the number three was also sacred to the pre-Christian Celts.

Patrick's words are like iron heated on the forge and hammered out in showers of sparks into tools to be used to tear down what is old and build up what is new in human hearts. They call upon all Nature with a resounding power and declare the oneness of God, the only Creator.

Patricius (in Latin), Padraig (in Irish) or Patrick (in English), if not the first, was certainly the greatest early teacher of Christianity in Ireland. He was ordained as a bishop in 432. The Roman church did not reach to the British Isles until more than a century later, so the Christianity which took hold in Ireland was very much Patrick's version.

Patrick was a bold, early teacher of the ecological holiness practiced by the original free Celtic church until it was overwhelmed by the cruel military hierarchies and compulsory religions of Rome and later England. To the Celtic church, Nature was not sinful, but sacred. Perhaps this is why the Celtic cross most commonly appears, not alone, but embracing or embraced by a circle, the symbol of the Earth, the Cosmos, and Nature.

To the early saints like Patrick, Brigid, and Columba; the poor and the weak, the earth, sea and sky, all animals and creatures alike were filled with a sacred light. Nature was as true a teacher as scripture. John Scotus Erigena, "the Irish-born Scot" born around 810, taught that "Scripture and Nature are the two shoes of Christ." Erigena's books were declared to be heresy and ordered burned by the Pope in 1225. This only increases our admiration for him.

In an age when women were seriously oppressed and celibacy was everywhere else required for the religious life, Celtic priests and monks often lived together in the same monasteries and were allowed to marry. Women—Saint Brigid for one—were even ordained as bishops.

In an age when very few could read, the Celtic Church considered literacy absolutely essential to the spiritual life. The Celtic monasteries copied in their scriptoria, and preserved in their libraries, not only Christian documents, but so-called "pagan" Greek manuscripts of history and philosophy, a practice that was anathema to the Roman church.

In an age when war was a universal practice, Patrick was an advocate of peaceful change. He converted the Irish to Christianity with magical, not military power, without fielding a single soldier, much less an army. When the monk Columcille rashly gathered his kinsmen together to avenge the death of a family member, a battle followed. As a result, Columcille was excommunicated and banished from Ireland to Iona, where he changed his ways and founded a monastery which still stands.

In an age when slavery was a universal practice—supported by scripture—Patrick fiercely opposed it. Thomas Cahill declares Patrick to be the first human being in history to challenge and condemn the ownership of one human being by another. His youthful years spent as a slave taught him the utter cruelty of it, and after Patrick, no greater opponent of human bondage would appear in the British Isles until the 17th century. Patrick also fiercely opposed, and totally eliminated in Ireland, the practice of human sacrifice, which was a regular religious ritual among the pre-Christian Celts.

The Celtic church preserved ancient learning and peaceful human values while the Dark Ages fell upon Europe, and the continent tore itself apart. Irish monks, male and female, carried these values carefully and lovingly forward until they could again be spread through the world.

What can Patrick and the Celtic Church teach us? They can teach us these truths: It is evil for men to gain the whole world and lose their souls. It is evil for humans to own other humans, or to sacrifice them to human purposes or to angry, vengeful gods. It is evil and corrupting to the human spirit to practice war.

They can teach us that it is good and essential to the spiritual life to be literate and to study the ancient wisdom. It is good for men and women to marry and live a consecrated life together, and it is good for women to have a status equal to that of men. They can teach us that Nature and all creatures are not vile and fallen, but sacred and holy.

Congregations of faithful, dedicated and jolly human beings can preserve and protect these sacred truths even as the whole world around them is caught up in chaos and destruction; and such faithful communities can carry these truths through to flourish again.

This is the marvelous heritage of Patrick and the Celtic church. May it live.

In times when human oppression, the desecration of Nature, the worship of violence, and the abandonment of ancient learning begin to rule, a Dark Age follows. We fool ourselves if we think that such times may not come again. They well may come again sooner than we think. Yet, whenever such a Dark Age comes to pass, faithful human beings can bind themselves together in faithful communities to protect, nurture and carry forward the immortal, invisible light.

Then, the spirit of Patrick will be with them, with the strength of heaven, light of sun, radiance of moon, splendour of fire, speed of lightning, swiftness of wind, depth of sea, stability of earth, and firmness of rock.

And, undoubtedly, with a good measure of merry-making.

THE DEVIL'S INSTRUMENT

The fiddle has long been known as the Devil's instrument. The link between the Devil and dance goes back at least to early Christians who condemned the Dionysian rites of drinking and dancing to stringed instruments. Remember, Pan had hooves and horns. The link between the Devil and the fiddle dates to the emergence of the violin as the favorite accompaniment to folk dancing in the 15th and 16th centuries. In the early 19th century the violinist Nicolo Paganini, with his long hair and fierce virtuosity, so astounded European audiences that they declared he must have made a pact with Satan himself to be able to play as he did; and the church even refused Paganini's burial in consecrated ground for years after his death. The fiddle was for Saturday night, but the pipe organ alone was for Sunday morning.

In Norway there is the myth of *Fanitullen* with a hoofed fiddler playing at a dire, bloody wedding. In Ireland it's *Devil among the Tailors* and *Go to the Devil and Shake Yourself*. In America, one of the wildest old dance tunes, still played by fiddlers today, is *The Devil's Dream*. Stephen Vincent Benet's 1925 poem *The Mountain Whippoorwill* rhapsodized on the legendary diabolical powers of fiddlers. The Charlie Daniels band burnished the legend in 1979 with *The Devil Went Down to Georgia*, wherein Johnny the fiddler and Old Scratch face off in a Faustian duel in which Johnny wins a gold fiddle and saves his soul while the Devil skulks away empty-handed.

I am saying all this as the prelude to a true confession; and here it is: I love to steal into the quiet church when no one else is around and fire up my fiddle. I love to play the sad, sweet notes of *Neil Gow's Lament* while salty tears wet the strings. I love to blast the wild, sweaty cadences of *The Morpeth Rant* to echo from the empty walls and pews, while the early or late light pours yellow and red through the stained glass windows. I love to stand before the portrait of the dour old preacher Jonathan Fisher and play for him *The Devil's Dream*. He sometimes seems to smile a little, noting perhaps that I am not a great fiddler; but also acknowledging that no one could love it more.

Could the music we love be etched deep in our genes? For 40 years I have gone through books and books of old fiddle tunes to try them out one by one. Most leave me cold, but a few set my soul on fire. When I find these tunes at last, I never tire of playing them. Are these the ones my ancestors loved? Are they imprinted in the very cells of my body? Some of these melodies are hundreds, nay, thousands of years old. They were the first language of the human race, chanting thoughts too deep for words. They were sung on the plains of Africa. They enlivened the Neolithic huts of Europe and echoed off the monolithic stone circles of Brittany and Ireland, owned by no one and loved by everyone, polished and passed down to us to drive the Devil from the door.

Just listen to the stories they tell: *The Boys of Blue Hill, Haste to the Wedding* and *Smash the Windows. The Priest in His Boots, Hunting the Hare* and *Bobbing for Eels. One Bottle More, Because He Was a Bonny Lad, The Ladies Delight* and *The Soldiers Joy.*

Saturday night always dawns Sunday morning. The Devil is

only the mythic embodiment of our corporate fear and hate. There is no reason to believe that the Devil will win your soul if you love the fiddle. No, there is far more reason to believe he will steal your soul if you hate it.

FAMILY

Karen Armstrong's biography of the Buddha begins: "One night a young man called Siddhatta Gotama walked out of his comfortable home... in the foothills of the Himalayas and took to the road. We are told that he was twenty-nine years old. His father was one of the leading men... and had surrounded Gotama with every pleasure he could desire. He had a wife and a son who was only a few days old, but Gotama had felt no pleasure when the child was born. He had called the little boy Rahula or 'fetter': the baby he believed would shackle him to a way of life that had become abhorrent... Gotama's parents wept... Before he left, Siddhatta stole upstairs, took one last look at his sleeping wife and son, and crept away without saying goodbye." (*Buddha* by Karen Armstrong, Penguin, 2001)

When Jesus called his disciples he told them to leave their jobs and families and follow him. Peter and Andrew were told to leave fishing. James and John were also told to leave their fishing and even leave their father who was counting on them for help. Peter said to Jesus, "Look we have left everything and followed you."

Jesus replied, "There is no one who has left house or brothers, sisters or fathers or children or fields for my sake who will not receive a hundredfold..." (Mk 10:28ff) One man said to Jesus, "I will follow you anywhere, but first let me go bury my father and say goodbye to my people at home." Jesus said to him, "Let the dead bury their own dead. No one who puts his hand to the plow and then looks back is fit for the kingdom...." (Lk 10:57) Another time he said, "Whoever comes to me and does not hate father and mother, wife and children, brothers and sisters, yes, even life itself, cannot be my disciple." (Lk 14:26)

What is going on here? In both East and West, the highest expression of the spiritual life has long been the renouncing of family and society as though such ties and affections were evil. Solitude, celibacy and self-deprivation were seen as the highest good. Jesus never married. Buddha left his wife, child and family. Paul never married, and considered loving partnership to be a considerably lower state than celibacy.

Organized religion has long called the faithful away from family and into the cloistered life, separated from the opposite sex and from the young, and taking strict vows of poverty, chastity and obedience. A modern secular variation of the monastic model is the employee of a large corporation who is utterly devoted to its values, putting them above all else, a modern monk who rises early in the morning to praise the corporation and returns late at night to give the spouse and the children a perfunctory blessing.

There are some huge problems with this model. Aside from the fact that most tribes and nations trace their descent from ancient divine Mothers and Fathers and holy families; aside from the fact that the family household, not the monastic cubicle, is the basic unit of all societies; aside from the fact that humans have lived and loved in families since the beginning and found there the highest expression of humanity; aside from all this there is an even greater flaw in the monkish model of saints through the ages. It is a dead end. If everyone were to do unto others as the celibate saints do, the human enterprise would come to an end rather abruptly due to a lack of any more humans. In fact, this is exactly what happened to the Shakers.

So, let us now praise, not the pious celibate monks and nuns, but the loyal mothers and fathers, daughters and sons and loving partners who create, nurture and bind together various holy families all over the earth without being canonized or enshrined. Let us praise earthly loving families and partners who provide a more authentic model of the real incarnated, embodied heavenly life than all the cloisters ever built.

Having said that, we must quickly add that anyone who has lived for long in a kinship or extended family enterprise (this latter includes churches) will not be too quick to condemn those who have chosen to flee to the safer and simpler refuge of the monastery. They have their reasons, and who hasn't thought of doing the same now and then? The family can be heaven, or hell, on earth.

"The family:" said Erma Bombeck, "we were a strange little band of characters trudging through life sharing diseases and toothpaste, coveting one another's desserts, hiding shampoo, borrowing money, locking each other out of our rooms, inflicting pain, and kissing to heal it in the same instant, loving, laughing, defending, and trying to figure out the common thread that bound us all together."

Squabbles over dessert and toothpaste may morph into arguments over politics and religion as anyone who has been to a family reunion or Thanksgiving dinner can testify. Most large families include members as different from each other as Yankee fans and Red Sox fans, liberals and conservatives, or Republicans and Democrats.

Humorist Dave Barry put it this way: "The Democrats seem to be basically nicer people, but they have demonstrated time and again that they have the management skills of celery. They're the kind of people who'd stop to help you change a flat, but would somehow manage to set your car on fire. I would be reluctant to trust them with a Cuisinart, let alone the economy. The Republicans on the other hand, would know how to fix your tire, but they wouldn't bother to stop because they want to be on time for Ugly Pants Night at the country club." Perhaps this is why George Burns said, "Happiness is having a large loving caring close-knit family in another city."

The failures for any family, household, tribe or church start when its members cannot get beyond their own individual needs to the needs of the whole. Fulfillment in the family comes in serving each other, and something greater. Family members must serve each other or the family will be overwhelmed by forces from within. But, a family must also serve something greater than itself or it will be overcome by forces from outside. It must serve God, not mammon, or it will perish.

In some way we are all seeking the One Big Happy Family, the First Family, the Primal Family, the Holy Family that can happen when unhappy and unholy families are willing to break out of their aloneness and self absorption, their counting up of wrongs done to them by others and turn themselves loose to be re-invented, re-incorporated, re-incarnated into a Greater Body for a Greater Good.

It is written, "Seek and you will find."

You might want to start looking in the kitchen first.

MONEY

We don't often talk about money on Sunday morning, except during the offering and the occasional stewardship message. Yet I'll bet most of us think about money nearly every hour of every day, including Sunday morning, and even in the dark hours of the night. I do, and I know I'm not the only one. Our parsonage is situated about 100 feet from a 24-hour ATM machine, and if you wonder whether people are thinking about money in the middle of the night, let me tell you, they are.

In the big picture, the modest salary that I receive puts me among the wealthiest people, not only in the world today, but in the history of civilization. By the standards of the time of Jesus, every single one of us is richer than royalty.

There is a debate raging in churches all over America today on the whole matter of faith and wealth. It was nicely covered in *Time* magazine in an article entitled "Does God Want You To Be Rich?" The lead picture was a rendering of DaVinci's famous painting of God's hand reaching out from heaven to touch Adam's. But in this case, instead of reaching out with the eternal life-giving touch, God is handing Adam a bundle of hundred dollar bills.

Time goes on to describe numerous churches that preach the "Prosperity Gospel." One is Lakewood Church in Houston led by mega-pastor and best-selling author, Joel Osteen, who preaches that "one of God's top priorities is to shower blessings on Christians in this lifetime—and the corollary assumption is that one of the worst things a person can do is to expect anything less." One parishioner is quoted as saying, "God does not want me to be a run-of-the-mill person... It's a new day God has given me! I'm on my way to a six figure income!" According to *Time*, three of the four biggest churches in the country preach the Prosperity Gospel, and hundreds of others incorporate aspects of it. Naturally, they all claim the Bible backs them up.

So how did Jesus himself feel about wealth and poverty?

Let's take a brief look not only at Jesus himself, but his mother, father, aunt, uncle, cousin, and brother who made up one of the most remarkable families ever seen in history or legend. They presented a revolutionary overturning of the ancient conviction that wealth was a sign of God's favor, and poverty a sign of God's condemnation. They turned the old, weary world upside down.

Miriam or "Mary" was a pregnant teenager who sang, "God has put down the mighty, he has filled the hungry with good things and sent the rich away empty-handed." Her fiance, Yusef or "Joseph," stayed by her and helped raise the son, not his own, teaching him the trade of carpentry, a trade not known for making a man wealthy, as any carpenter will tell you.

Then there was Mary's cousin Elizabeth who ecstatically cried out "Blessed are you among women" when she heard that Mary was pregnant. Elizabeth was married to Zacaria or "Zechariah," a quiet, devout man who had a menial job at the temple, also a sure ticket to a life of poverty.

Elizabeth and Zechariah's only son Yohanna, or "John" the Baptist, was a cousin to Jesus and preached "He who has two coats, let him share with him who has none, and he who has food, let him do likewise." John was imprisoned without trial and executed by the Roman puppet governor Herod for publicly condemned Herod's immorality.

Yeshua or "Jesus," the son of Mary and Joseph preached (Luke 6:20ff), "Blessed are you poor, for yours is the kingdom of God... But woe to you that are rich, for you have received your consolation." Jesus told the rich young ruler that he lacked one thing. "Sell what you have and give it to the poor," he said, "for it is harder for a rich man to enter into the kingdom of heaven than for a camel to go through the eye of a needle." Jesus, as we all know, was executed by the authorities of the Roman colonial government with the consent of the religious establishment after a mock trial.

Then there was Yacub or "James" who was also the son of Mary and Joseph and brother to Jesus according to tradition. In the Letter of James we hear resounding echoes of his brother's preaching. I will quote James on wealth and poverty at some length:

"Let the lowly brother boast in his exaltation, and the rich in his humiliation, because like the flower of the field he will pass away" (James 1:10).

"Listen, my beloved... Has not God chosen those who are poor in the world to be rich in faith... But you have dishonored the poor man. Is it not the rich who oppress you? Is it not they who drag you into court? (2:5ff)

"Come now, you rich, weep and howl for the miseries that are coming upon you. Your riches have rotted and your garments are moth-eaten. Your gold and silver have rusted, and their rust will be evidence against you and will eat your flesh like fire... See the wages of the laborers who mowed your fields which you have kept back by fraud... You have lived on the earth in luxury and in pleasure; you have fattened your hearts in a day of slaughter. You have condemned, you have killed the righteous man (5:1-6)."

James the brother of Jesus was assassinated by the religious elite, the scribes and the Pharisees.

The fierce vision of this remarkable family, which informs the entire New Testament, leaves little wiggle room on the matter of riches. An entirely new view of wealth is presented, and an evolutionary breakthrough in human consciousness. Riches are no longer the sign of God's favor as in former times, but a major liability in the kingdom of heaven.

It's natural to hear the preaching of Jesus and his family as harsh and condemning, particularly if we are ultimately counting on money to save us or to make us happy. It's natural to think that maybe they were just angry because they were poor. Maybe they were jealous of those who had more. But, when we hear them say, "Blessed are you poor" and "Woe to you rich," it's good to remember that "blessed" simply means "happy" and "woe" means "sad." Maybe they were on to something much deeper than anger or jealousy.

Research has shown again and again that, after a certain point of basic security is reached, ever more wealth does not mean ever more happiness or contentment: Quite the contrary. It means ever more trouble and heartache. You think Donald Trump is a happy and contented man? Then, baby, you're fired.

The truth is that wealth causes poverty. It causes poverty of the body for the poor, and poverty of the soul for the wealthy.

Knowing this, the ancient Levitical code prescribed the time of Jubilee, when all debts were required to be forgiven and holdings of land were to be returned to the Lord. Likewise, the Indians of the Northwest coast had a tradition the whites called "potlatch" whereby the wealthiest of the tribe would periodically hold a ceremony to give away all that they had, until they were reduced to utter poverty.

"We make a living by what we get," said Winston Churchill, "but we make a life by what we give."

Invisible Hands

*

Dear Simon,

Your willingness to call me on my proposition that "wealth causes poverty" is refreshing, and I appreciate it. Your letter has stimulated me to review Bentham, Smith, and Mill whom I waded through unenthusiastically in college, and has also encouraged me to study Keynes and Galbraith whom I have not read before. This has been satisfying and I am grateful for your honorable and direct challenges to my admittedly rudimentary understanding of economics.

Before any response to your points, let me make some observations about ideology. There is a temptation to divide social philosophies into two camps, "conservative" and "liberal." This temptation is fine in an academic sense, but would be soon thwarted by a thorough self-examination which often reveals that we are each a little of both, thus complicating our desire to easily stereotype others.

I tend to think of myself as liberal in economics, since I believe there is more than enough to go around and that everyone can have a decent standard of living. On the other

185

hand, I do not believe that the government can enforce economic equality without risks to freedom, which would make me a conservative. Nor do I believe the unfettered "market" or "free enterprise" system can bring about economic justice on its own, which would make me a liberal, I suppose.

I am also liberal theologically and abhor creeds while supporting the separation between church and state. I tend to be socially conservative in that I believe in monogamy and marital fidelity, but also do not believe that the government ought to regulate sexual behavior between consenting adults, making me liberal. I do not think abortion after the first trimester is morally right, but further do not think that the government has any business regulating the right of a woman to decide whether or not to bear a child.

I have been a gun owner all my adult life, and do not think that the government should prevent adults never convicted of a crime from having reasonable means of self-protection, that is, firearms. Nor do I believe that the government should support a standing army as this inevitably leads to abuses such as military repression at home or military adventurism abroad. Is this liberal or conservative? It gets confusing.

But back to the proposition that wealth causes poverty. As you rightly pointed out, this statement must rest on a "zero-sum" model of economy. You presented the example of Henry Ford and the Model T, suggesting that Ford was actually creating wealth where there was none before by manufacturing something more valuable from resources that are less valuable, and that wealth could be continually expanded in this way.

For this "expanding" economic model to hold true through time, it would be necessary to show that there were no limits to such expansion of wealth. This would mean that resources would have to expand as well. Otherwise, a *point would be reached when the resources required for the manufacture and operation of myriads of Model Ts would be exhausted, and the economic growth based upon those resources would eventually collapse.*

For this expanding economic model to hold, it would further be necessary to show that the wealth or "standard of living" of all participants in this economic system, whether owners or laborers, would increase proportionately over time.

This model raises several questions in my mind. Modern physics holds that neither matter nor energy is either created or destroyed. On the contrary, the sum of matter and energy throughout the universe appears to remain constant: $E=mc$ squared.

On the ground, this means that neither the iron that is consumed in the construction of the Model T, nor the petroleum that is consumed in its operation, is unlimited. These are finite resources. They can be converted, but their sum cannot be increased. The earth is not producing any more iron or petroleum, as far as we know.

So, the wealth created by the production of the Model T depends upon the impoverishment of the planet's limited resources. This holds true with any economic model in which resources are consumed faster than they are produced. Wealth which depends on finite resources may increase temporarily, but when the resources are exhausted, wealth disappears and poverty follows.

Adam Smith wrote The Wealth of Nations before the extractive economy of the Industrial Revolution, which depended on non-renewable resources like coal and iron, superseded the agricultural economy, which depended on renewable resources like the soil, crops and livestock. As long as the fertility of the soil is continually improved, which is possible to a point, an agricultural economy could increase wealth, but again, there is a limit to what the soil can produce.

Here is another challenge to the expanding economy model: If wealth could actually continue to increase without limit, all other things being equal, eventually everyone would be wealthy, or at least not poor. Historically, this has not proven to be the case. For all the wealth of nations, there is still massive poverty world-wide, and the gap between rich and poor is widening.

(As an aside here, many argue that poverty is caused by over-population. But there is much concrete evidence that the contrary is the case. That is, that poverty causes over-population. Statistics show that the higher the standard of living, the lower the rate of population increase. In the U.S.—the richest country in the world—the fertility rate has been dropping for decades as education and standard of living rises.)

But, back to wealth causing poverty. There are millions who work brutally hard all of their lives and end up destitute, while others live a life of comparative leisure and end up wealthy. Who ever got rich cutting sugar cane, picking apples or raking blueberries 50, 60 or 70 hours a week? As Merle Haggard put it, "Work your fingers to the bone. What do you get? Bony fingers."

If the expanding economy model is invalid, then there must be other reasons why some are wealthy and others remain dirt poor. Perhaps the labor of the hard-working poor does not make them worthy to become wealthy, though this apparently works for the rich and directly challenges our sense of fairness. Perhaps the poor are displeasing to God and so are punished with poverty, though this runs counter to the testimony of the gospels which repeat, "Blessed are the poor..."

Or perhaps it is something else—and this is the basis of my contention that wealth causes poverty. Perhaps the *wealthy know that no economy can expand forever and so are tempted to preserve their wealth by using its power, wittingly or unwittingly, to ensure that they (we) will gain more and more wealth at the expense of others who work just as hard or even harder, yet must remain in poverty for us to get rich.*

We do have a word from Adam Smith on this: "Civil government..." he wrote, "is in reality instituted for the defence of the rich against the poor, or of those who have some property against those who have none at all."

And, we have a word from James, the brother of Jesus, who wrote: "Is it not the rich who oppress you, is it not they who drag you into court?" James 2:6. (See also Luke 6:20-25, James 2:14-17 and 5:1-6)

As mentioned above, I don't feel that either government or the market have proven completely effective as yet (in our country, at least) in eliminating poverty. It is up to us to find the answer.

That's probably more than enough on the subject of wealth and poverty. I look forward to your response. Maybe we could get together over coffee or lunch sometime to talk about it.

Sincerely yours,

Rob

(Since this exchange, Simon has become actively involved in engineering micro-loans in a poor Central American country.)

INTELLIGENT EVOLUTION

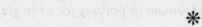

You may be bored to tears with the endless debate between "evolution" and "intelligent design." Tears might be good here. I find the debate about as fascinating as a barroom brawl over the comparative merits of the Yankees and the Red Sox. What's the problem here? Evolution and intelligent design are far more alike than they are different, like the left hand and the right hand. Though it is good to see ultimate questions debated in the public forum, the truth is that there is no convincing proof yet for either side. This debate is as fruitless as the one about the chicken and the egg. Everywhere we turn our eyes we see ample evidence for both evolution and intelligent design.

As suggested before, intelligent design could engender evolution just as easily as evolution could engender intelligent design. Could not a cosmic intelligence design evolution? Does not evolution need a Source from which to evolve? These two are the yin and yang of the Creation, the right and the left, the male and the female: dualities that will never be completely resolved. What's more, the noisy debate about them agitates the adults, frightens the children, and startles the chickens, providing still more evidence that people don't have enough to do.

Furthermore, the whole uproar may be simply another smoke-screen put down to cover the plutocrats' plundering of the public commonwealth. While our pockets are being picked we get lost in finger-pointing and hand-wringing over the meaning of shadows thrown by the camp-fire on the wall of the cave. Our hands are better used helping those who suffer the vagaries of Nature and the inequities of economics world-wide.

It's time for a dose of reality. If you think the last two winters in Maine were tough, just watch. As fuel, food and medicine prices soar, prepare for reports of the poor and elderly starving and freezing on the back roads in your own home town. It won't matter then whether they were intelligently designed or whether they evolved. Don't look to the minions of government to help here. They're fiddling while the world burns. We are called to service, not stridence. Pay forward to your local church, community organization, and food-pantry. You too may need them.

We will leave it up to others to speculate which of the following are the result of intelligent design and which are not: June bugs that fall over on their backs and can't get up; Raspberry seeds that get stuck in the teeth: smoke that blows in your eyes no matter where you sit around the fire; burdocks and your cat; porcupines and your dog; Boston's Big Dig; the Style section of the *New York Times*; the radio tower on Awanadjo; and lastly, the ghastly war on terrorism.

LIFE AND DEATH

The following are excerpts from memorial services for young people whose parents and families were left with the agonies, the sorrows and the questions that such untimely deaths inevitably leave in their aftermath.

When death comes to someone before her time, when the younger die before the older, when someone good and kind suffers, we may rightfully rage or wonder "Why, why?" We may say, "It's so unfair." We may blame God, or someone else so as to have a target for our sadness or anger, like sticking pins in a voodoo doll to hurt someone else as we are hurt. Then, it's worth remembering that Rabbi Kushner's classic volume on suffering was not titled "*Why Bad Things Happen to Good People.*" It was "*When Bad Things Happen to Good People.*"

When bad things happen what brings the healing? Does fear? Anger? Bitterness? Blaming God or the Universe or someone else? Voodoo? No. What brings the healing is love and forgiveness and grace. Love, most of us can do, sometimes better, sometimes worse. Forgiveness may be harder. Here's a lesson in fundamental forgiveness I learned from our old dog Quoddy. Quoddy was a big black dog who had a habit of falling asleep on the floor right in the way of where we usually walked. One dark night I tripped and fell over him in the front room of the parsonage. It hurt me a little, but it probably hurt him a lot more. He jumped up with a yelp and ran out of the room as I picked myself up. While I picked myself up and stood there cursing and fuming at him, I soon felt his cold nose nuzzling into my hand. He had come back in the dark to forgive me, and I felt that feral forgiveness wash over me and change me.

Now, grace is the healing that comes freely from the Universe following forgiveness. An old friend of ours used to say "Grace may come from above or it may come from below; it may come crooked or it may come straight; it may come early or it may come late: but it comes." I'd add that grace can come on two legs or four, or even more.

Forgiveness makes it possible to go on when bad things happen. Yes, bad things happen to people, maybe more than their share, but they can forgive and go on. If we cannot forgive, like Marley's ghost we are burdened with more and more chains of pain forged in life, until we can no longer move. Forgiveness cuts those chains and let's them fall so we can walk and live free again.

"Dead, I say? There is no death, only a change of worlds."
—From Chief Seattle at the signing of the
Port Huron treaty in 1855.

Why do we banish the dead whom we love to some far-away heaven or hell, beyond the reach of our needs and affections? Why do we put the dead in sealed boxes and vaults in the ground and place heavy stones upon their graves? Why do we stop speaking to them or consulting them? With all of our Bibles and prayers and rituals are we still afraid of them? Do we think those who cared about us and loved us in life care any less after they have died? Why should they be exiled from us? What good does this do for us, or them?

Belief in an after-life is ridiculed as irrational by some, but there is no more rational evidence that there is not an after-life than that there is. I find ample evidence that death is not the end, and a complete lack of any convincing evidence that it is.

Why? Science shows that matter and energy are neither created nor destroyed, but are constantly changing form. Physics demonstrates unseen dimensions of space and time that nevertheless exist and influence what we can see. The body does not disappear at death, it simply changes. It returns to the elements to be reconfigured.

Story, scripture and song through the ages, and nearly all religions, affirm an existence after death. Those who have returned from what we call "near-death experiences" report a real state beyond this present life. I would be the first to say that we should reject charlatans who claim to contact the dead (and get paid for doing so), or theologians and priests who claim that we go far away to heaven or hell or purgatory or limbo when we die (and also get paid for saying so). I have little patience with such groundless pronouncements.

But maybe it is time for us to rediscover the ancient bridge between this world and the other. The way we are to those who have died should be for each of us to determine for ourselves in a way that benefits the living, and if possible the dead. As a teaching to our children, instead of banishing the dead from our lives to our endless sorrow and grief; maybe it's time to treat them the way we would be treated: to do to them as we would have others do to us: Not to banish and forget those who have died; and certainly not to let them hurt us or do us wrong, but to love and forgive them.

It's time to speak and listen openly and willingly to those we loved who have died, while we remain among the living; to remember and recall them at tender times, so that when we go, not so very far away, to be with them, we can be cherished, loved, heard and forgiven, as we have cherished, loved, heard, and forgiven.

Dead, I say? There is no death, only a change.

We talk daily about death in hushed voices with long faces, painfully aware of its reality. We stand by the casket with our hands clasped over our vitals as thought to protect them. We read the obituaries with our morning coffee, and see the evidence of the horrible toll of war and rage and accident and disease taken by the one St. Francis of Assisi called "our Brother Death, whom no man escapeth." Even the animals have an awareness of their own death: like the dog who wanders away to die or the elephant who does the same and is mourned by others of its kind.

In our time, the young and not-so-young may try to overcome their fear of death by driving too fast without a seat-belt or jumping out of airplanes or climbing Mount Everest; taking risks to confront and challenge their own death. Others who are not inclined to bungee-jumping may prefer to read their holy book and its interpreters and expositors trying to convince themselves and others that they will go to heaven if they only believe enough.

There is a multi-million dollar industry presently encouraging the fearful throngs that they will not really die if they utter the right words in the right order or perform certain ritual acts that will somehow overturn the primal knowledge that we all die. It is the same industry that priest-craft has been engaged in for ages. I would be untruthful if I did not say that I am deeply suspicious of this sort of industry, making money from the fear of death.

We know we will die. That is sure enough. But what's next? Some, like Orthodox Judaism and a few tribal religions, say that death is final. But the human race largely holds that death is not the end: a change, but not a conclusion. My father died in 1967 of a painful heart failure, but I have the abiding memory of his final words to sustain me. He said, "Either the pain is gone, or I am gone," showing me that at the moment of death he moved beyond the pain of life.

Nature, too, shows that change is more real than death. A

great tree, as it nears the end of its own life, begins to lose limbs, to rot, and then to become food for insects, fungi and lichen. One day the wind overcomes the trunk and it falls to the ground. Immediately it begins to enrich the soil with more life. At what moment in time did this tree become dead? It never did.

Of course, there is natural death and there is un-natural death. The death of an elder after a long life is natural and can be accepted with joy. The deaths of the young and the innocent by hunger or disease or wars that could be prevented by human effort are un-natural events and should be received with deep sadness and a fierce determination to prevent such needless deaths.

In First Corinthians 15 the apostle Paul offers a long, technical, and frankly (in one preacher's opinion) inscrutable sermon about resurrection. But he concludes it with some stirring words. "I will tell you a mystery. We shall not all sleep, but we shall all be changed in a moment, in the twinkling of an eye... For the trumpet shall sound and the dead shall be raised imperishable, and we shall be changed... O death, where is thy victory? O death, where is thy sting?" Paul repeats here the nearly universal conviction that death is not the end.

Would it be better if we knew what was going to happen to us after we die or could control it by what we do while alive, as some claim with talk of who's going to be "raptured" or go to heaven and who's not? I do not believe that humans, who cannot even accurately predict the weather two days ahead, are equipped to determine or control what will happen in eternity to ourselves or anyone else. Even if we could, it would be like a vending machine: you put in certain things while you live and certain things come down the chute when you die. This is not faith, friends, this is commerce. Far better to trust God to do the right thing in life, and in death.

Isaiah said, "(M)y thoughts are not your thoughts, neither are your ways my ways, says the Lord. For as the heavens are higher than the earth, so are my ways higher than your ways, and my thoughts than your thoughts."

Jesus said, "Of that day or that hour no one knows, only the Father."

This ancient wisdom about the limits of human understanding led to the much-maligned doctrine of predestination (see essay above) which held that nothing we can do in this life will determine what happens to us or to others in eternity. Only God can determine that. We don't know who is redeemed and who is not. This leaves us in the position of doing good simply because it is the right thing to do, not because it will gain us a golden crown studded with diamonds or a mansion in the sky with silver plumbing fixtures some day—and what good would such things be in heaven anyway?

You probably know the old story about the newcomer to heaven being shown around by St. Peter, but it fits so well here that I can't resist telling it again. "Over here," says St. Pete to the newcomer, "you'll find the Buddhists—you can hear them chanting. Farther along here are the Hindus. Over here are the Muslims—you can hear them praying. A little farther along are the Unitarians—you can hear them asking questions. Over here are the Quakers—you can't hear them at all. And over here are the Baptists, but you'll have to be quiet, because they think they're the only ones here."

So, it was refreshing to read about elderly evangelical Christian battle-axe Billy Graham's new-found humility when asked not long ago if he thinks heaven is closed to non-Christians. "Those are decisions only the Lord will make," he said. "I believe the love of God is absolute... and I think he loves everybody regardless of what label they have."

Roman poet Publius Syrus said: "The fear of death is more to be dreaded than death itself." I have found that if anything can overcome death, it is not fear and it is not certainty. It is love. Love is the universal medicine to relieve pain, suffering, fear and death. At every graveside gathering we see an outpouring of love for the one who died, regardless of whether he or she was the sweetest of saints or the sorriest of scoundrels.

There is a deeply endearing natural human wisdom at work when we gather to remember someone who has died. Just by standing there by the open grave we are quietly insisting that love will have the last word. If such poor human love comes pouring out at the time of death, how much more will the pure Creator's love pour out at the time of death and beyond?

I believe that we were brought forth, not by some meaningless, purposeless and random accident, but by a loving Creator out of a deep, holy will and desire for us to be. I believe that we are loved by our Creator while we live, even though it may sometimes be a truly tough love. I believe that we will be received in love by that same Creator when we die. And I believe that we do best when we don't try to second-guess or control the next life, but put our faith in the Creator in this life, and love the heavens and the earth and everything in them all the time: stars and skunks, saints and scoundrels.

Given all this, I believe that when our hour comes at last—an hour which no one can know but God—then we will go out in joy and be led forth in peace, the mountains and the hills will break into singing, and all the trees of the field will clap their hands.

"Under the wide and starry sky, dig the grave
and let me lie.
Glad did I live and gladly die, and I laid me down
with a will.
This be the verse you grave for me: 'Here he lies
where he longed to be,
Home is the sailor, home from the sea, and the hunter home
from the hill.'"
—From "Requiem" by Robert Louis Stevenson

Stan was a hunter, and for a certain kind of person, life will forever be a hunt. Hunters set out in the early morning to seek, to find, and to bring home what is needful for their own nourishment and the nourishment of those they love. In their hunting day by day they learn by heart the lay of the land, the livelihoods and habits and the natural wisdom of the game they seek. It becomes part of them. Few know the truths Nature teaches better than the hunter. Few care more for the lives of the creatures they follow and study than the hunter. Few are better friends and defenders of Nature than hunters. Throughout their lives good hunters increase in their knowledge, respect and reverence for their quarry and for the land, field and forest they roam. Good hunters are merciful to their quarry, and have compassion for them in their dying. Good hunters leave no scars or refuse upon the land. Good hunters share their game with others, particularly those who cannot hunt. Of course, there are good and bad hunters; but there are also good and bad plumbers, bankers, doctors, environmentalists, politicians and (heaven knows) preachers. Even today, Stan is still a hunter. This is the man we remember.

To Stan's son Mac: I hope you will not be too embarrassed if I speak to you directly for just a moment. I lost my father when I was only a little older than you, at a time when I thought he had taught me everything I would ever want to learn from him. I have felt his loss deeply in the nearly 40 years since he died. But something remarkable, and far greater than the loss, has gradually come to pass during that time. My conversations with my father did not end when he died. They continued, and they continue to this day. Nearly every day I remember something he said to me. Just yesterday he was saying, "Son, you can call me from anywhere if you're in trouble, just don't call me from jail." When I am proud of something I have done, I feel his pride in what I did as though he were still with me. And of course he is. It's just that he's no longer beside me, he's inside me. When I'm in trouble, if I listen, his voice speaks the very words I need to hear. The distance between my father and me is in some ways less now than it was when he was alive. I believe, Matt, that you may one day discover the same, that your father is not ever farther away from you in the passing of days and years, but that he is ever nearer; and that he will always have something more to give you and teach you when you need it most.

To those who loved Stan: Such an illness and too early death are surely a great and deep sorrow. It would be tempting to find someone to blame for such a loss—the Creator, the Universe, the doctors, or even Stan himself. But, every life on earth is sooner or later touched by tragedy, and the sooner the redeeming power is found in Stan's life as he lived it and as he gave it up, the sooner the lives of those who loved him will begin to heal and be ready again to live and love more strongly with new knowledge of the uncertainty and shortness of life. It can be like coming home from the hunt without the quarry we were seeking, but with something entirely different and fully as good, the bracing sight of the beauty of turning leaves, a new sense of the Creator working in the world, a new vision of the holy wisdom embodied in living and dying, a new conviction of the fundamental goodness of the life of every creature lived the best it could, on foot or hoof or fin or wing.

"Home is the hunter, home from the hill." Stan's body returns now to the ground, earth to earth, its hunting over. But his spirit is still ranging far and wide over fields and mountains way beyond our sight, and in the quiet times in the hearts of those who loved him—if they are willing—he will surely, steadily and faithfully return again and again, bringing back the game that is needful for the nourishment of their spirits.

In *The Immense Journey* Loren Eiseley recounts waking from a nap in a glade far in the woods to "...see the dust motes of wood pollen in a long shaft of light, and there on an extended branch sat an enormous raven with a red and squirming nestling in his beak. The sound that awoke me was the outraged cries of the nestling's parents who flew helplessly in circles about the clearing. The sleek black monster was indifferent to them. He threw his head back, then whetted his beak on the dead branch and sat still. Out of all of that woodland a soft sound of complaint began to rise. Into the glade fluttered small birds of a half dozen varieties drawn by the outcries of the tiny parents.

"No one dared attack the raven, but they cried there in some instinctive common misery, the bereaved and the unbereaved. The glade filled with the soft rustling of their cries. He, the black bird at the heart of life, sat on there, glistening in the common light, formidable, unmoving, unperturbed, untouchable.

"It was then I saw a judgment upon life that was not passed by men. It was the judgment of life against death. I will never see it again so forcefully presented. I will never hear it again in notes so tragically prolonged. In the midst of protest, they forgot the violence. The crystal note of a song sparrow lifted hesitantly in the hush... the song passing from one bird to another, doubtfully at first, as though some evil thing were being slowly forgotten. Till suddenly they took heart and sang from many throats joyously together as birds sing. They sang because life is sweet and sunlight beautiful, under the shadow of the raven, for they were the singers of life, and not of death."

Now, the winged one has taken Emma. It had been hovering for a while; her friends and family saw its shadow and knew it was there, but it was too powerful and relentless to be cajoled or driven away. The horror is real, the tragedy is tremendous, of a beautiful young life devoured. The cold, hard finality is terrifying. We were shocked into speechless silence, filled with grief, anger, remorse, helplessness, sighing and tears.

But soon enough with the sighing and tears came the flowers and cookies and casseroles. Soon enough came the cards and embraces, and the house full of comfort. Soon enough the alchemy of friendship began to consume the dross of fear and rage with the fire of love and, by the grace of a God who knows the loss of a child, soon enough grief will be refined into hope

Soon enough, the song will begin again in these broken hearts, because we are singers of life, and not of death.

Let us pray.

Creator Spirit, all our relatives, all living things; Hear us.

See this one who has fallen. See this one who lately walked the earth and busied herself with flowers, with animals, with friends. See this one who made beauty around her. See this one who has fallen.

Spirit who brings all death back to life, hold her now, but do not let her be out of life long. Bring her back in the perfume of a flower, the stride of a four-legged creature, and the laughter of a friend. Do not let her be out of life long.

Creator Spirit, all our relatives, all living things; hear us.

Unto you, Creator of the heavens and the earth, we commend the spirit of our sister departed—earth to earth ashes to ashes, dust to dust, in sure and certain conviction of everlasting Life for all creatures.

And now may the One who can keep us from falling guide our feet in the path of wisdom, hope, and peace from this time forth and forever. Amen.

THE CROSS AND THE CIRCLE

It is well known that conquerors often try to erase all remnants of the religions they conquer. We know from archaeological evidence that the Jewish shrine at Bethel was built on the site of an earlier Canaanite shrine. We read in the Hebrew scriptures that Elijah slaughtered hundreds of the prophets of the ancient Canaanite fertility religion of Baal. We know also from archaeological evidence that many of the cathedrals of Europe were built on sacred sites of an older religion. Likewise in Latin America, colonial Spanish churches were built on the sites of the indigenous Aztec, Mayan, and Inca religions after their temples were destroyed and their priests were slaughtered. This seems to be the sad story from time immemorial. Conquerors do not drink from the wells their ancestors dug as much as they poison them.

There is evidence, however, that Celtic Christianity may have represented a departure from this horrible practice. Numerous scholars including Mary Low (*Celtic Christianity and Nature*, Edinburgh University Press, 1996), Alexander Carmichael, John Bell, Christopher Bamford and others have shown that early Irish Christians did not so much try to eliminate primal Celtic religion as incorporate it, adapt it, and build upon it; and they offer numerous fascinating examples from ancient Irish sources.

Prophets do not always seek to destroy the older religion. They may choose to refine it and improve it. Jesus did not try to destroy Judaism to start a new religion. He said that he came, not to overthrow the Jewish Law, but to fulfill it. He preserved and expanded the heart of the older religion, while discarding elements like ceremonial purity and dietary laws. When asked what was the greatest commandment, Jesus quoted the ancient tradition saying, "Love God with all your heart, soul, mind and strength; and love your neighbor as yourself." Likewise, St. Patrick vigorously maintained the ancient Celtic reverence for Nature and other ancient forms of practice and expression, but condemned the pre-Christian practices of slavery and human sacrifice.

Mary Low, borrowing from Australian scholar Harold Turner, describes the ancient spiritual wisdom, the old faith, preserved by the Celtic Christian church and surviving in many modern religions. I suspect that many of you will recognize this primal wisdom bubbling up in your own hearts: "A sense of kinship with all creatures, earth, plants, animals. A sense of creaturehood and humility in the face of greater powers, friendly and unfriendly. Little separation between the inhabitants of this world and the other, or between spirit and matter. A living and sacramental universe willing to share its powers and blessings in life and after death."

I would suggest a corollary: that to suppress or prohibit or seek to destroy these elements of primal spirituality toward Nature can create an imbalance in ourselves and our place in the universe—call it 'sin', if you will—and that to recover and incorporate these primal elements may lead to wholeness, or redemption, of us and the earth.

Certainly, to consolidate its own power and influence, orthodox Christianity actively interjected itself between the faithful and Nature. Traditional sacred places were obliterated and churches built upon them. Ancient guardians of sacred waters, trees, mountains and other places were replaced by 'saints' designated by the church. The dead have been sent far away to heaven or hell instead of staying nearby to teach and help. Intercessors and mediators between the living and the dead and between us and the Creator have been interposed by the church business just as the care of the dead has been taken over by the mortician business. Animals, plants and the earth have been demoted to inanimate, despised and fallen objects, allowing us to exploit them without going against established religion. "We have dimmed the light in the sacred grove," writes Annie Dillard; "we have gone from pan-theism to pan-atheism."

I believe that this ruthless conquering and spiritual colonization by established religion and the destruction of primal religion has brought us and the planet to our present precarious condition. Choose your own examples: global warming, extinction of species, materialism, industrialism, war, and the selling of the whole Creation as well as alienation, violence and the apotheosis of greed and competition.

Neither modern science alone, nor established religion alone can deliver us. It is time to return to the wells of our ancestors and drink their living water for our survival today, a truth that many of you already know instinctively. The truth that the whole Creation is alive and full of wisdom will eventually be reached by modern science, as it was by ancient religion.

Meanwhile, we can hold to the old faith as it still survives, passed on to us by Jesus, St. Patrick and so many others who did not seek to poison the ancient wells, but to purify and drink from them. If you are among the many who find the Holy in Nature as well as in church, you may be still practicing the primal religion, drinking living water from the wells dug by our ancestors, and you may understand the following vision of the Holy Creation given me one Winter evening as I pondered by the old Glenwood stove.

First, a germ of something in the mists of nothing,
Visible but invisible, there but not there,
A pulsing dent of light, of darkness, of death, of life,
Without weight or length or height or breadth,

All at once it wants; it wants a world,
A silent sounding out, growing, echoing, haloing, ringing,
An aura rounding outward,
And again and again, circling, rippling,
Center everywhere, circumference nowhere.

A crease, a seam, a wrinkle in time and space,
A horizon line arrives, faint extending,
Sharp-whetted, edging, knifing,
Slicing semi-circles of above, below,
A great single cell dividing into earth and heaven.

An axis, too, arises upward, drops downward,
Dividing dark from light, day from night, left from right.
Where axes cross a new heart beats weak,
Then strong, sending sap surging into the tree of life,
Roiling blood into the holy rood.

The beating heart a body grows,
A carnal cosmos, head high, legs low
Breasts flow, arms branch, each outreaches,
Starting the hearts of the thousand million creatures.
Hearts live, hearts laugh, hearts cry, hearts die.
Hearts heat, hearts beat, hearts break, hearts heal.

Why weep lonely, deaf to the echoes of these primal cries?
Why laugh alone while the morning stars smile,
And vast galaxies giggle and grieve together?

Why suffer in solitary silence while the wild flesh of earth
    and heaven
Is rent and torn and rent and then, again, knitted up whole
    and holy?

Hand the apple gladly back to the snake
Climb up the holy tree from whence we came,
To laugh, to weep, to mate, to eat, to meet our Maker,
While wild winds blow and Creation cradles rock,
To know the botanic Body of Creation as we know
    our own,
And know our own as the Body of Creation.

THE GHOST DANCE

Between 1870 and 1890, after years of inter-racial brutality, of whites seizing land that had belonged for millennia to indigenous people, after the virtual extermination of the huge herds of buffalo, out on the Great Plains Native American prophets had a vision of the world to come and began to preach among the tribes from California to the Great Basin to the Central and Northern Plains. Here is what they preached.

"Grandfather says when your friends die you must not cry. The dead are all alive again. You must not hurt anybody or do harm to anyone. You must not fight. Do right always; it will give you satisfaction in life. Jesus is now upon the earth. He appears like a cloud. I do not know when they will be here... when the time comes there will be no more sickness and everyone will be young again. Do not refuse to work for the whites and do not make any trouble with them until you leave them. Do not tell lies.

"I want you to dance. Make a feast and have food that everybody may eat. After this, wash in the water. That is all. You will receive good words from me again some time."

The dance was called the "Ghost Dance" and it swept many

of the tribes throughout the West with a millennial fervor, along with further prophecies that the buffalo and other animals would return, the whites would disappear, and the entire earth would turn green again.

Naturally, the white settlers and military authorities were alarmed at this mass movement with its large gatherings and ecstatic dancing, and tried to stop it. Tensions increased throughout the West, and on December 29th, 1890 troops of the Seventh Cavalry under General Nelson Miles surrounded and entered a Lakota camp near Wounded Knee, South Dakota to disarm the inhabitants. Shots were fired, and some 300 Lakota including over 200 unarmed women, children and elderly were cut down by Hotchkiss repeating guns fired by 'Christian' soldiers. Many of the Lakota fled and were pursued, shot in the back, and left to die or freeze to death on the open ground in an on-coming blizzard.

I tell this heartbreaking story for several reasons. First, because it happened one day after "Holy Innocents" on the church calendar marking the day when Herod slaughtered the innocent Jewish children; and every year at this season I am visited by the spirit of Wounded Knee.

Second, I tell this story because the massacre at Wounded Knee signaled the end of the old Native ways and, we fervently pray, the culmination of four centuries of atrocities committed between Europeans and Native Americans on this continent beginning in 1492.

And third, I tell this story because it is my conviction that the Ghost Dance which inspired these events represents a powerful melding of indigenous American and European spirituality, a joining of the sacred circle and the holy cross, a meeting of East and West which continues to this day across the entire continent and is gradually changing, and will continue to change, the faith and practice of America and the world.

The first two points few would dispute. I will try to convince you of the far more controversial third point. This will take some thinking outside the box (and outside the books.)

It goes without saying that I am no expert on indigenous spirituality, but I do know a thing or two about the history of both European and Native American religion and have been strongly influenced by both. I was born in Lakota country in the Black Hills of South Dakota. Family legend says that I was placed on the saddle of a Lakota horseman when I was a baby. I remember watching the Yakima with ropes tied around their waists dip-netting salmon from spindly platforms high above the Celilo Falls on the Columbia River before they were flooded by the Dalles Dam in 1957. And of course, the Passamaquoddy have influenced me for over 30 years.

Of the friendships with Native Americans that have shaped my faith, I will mention particularly Fox Tree from the Wampanoag, and Mary Bassett and the late Deanna Francis from the Passamaquoddy. For a great adventure with Deanna, I refer you to page 128 of my book, *Small Misty Mountain*.

Books that have shaped my understanding of Native American spirituality most powerfully include *The Ghost Dance Religion* by James Mooney, *Life and Traditions of the Red Man* by Joseph Nicolar, *Black Elk Speaks* by John Erdoes and Black Elk, *Lame Deer, Seeker of Visions* by John Fire Lame Deer, *Bury My Heart at Wounded Knee* by Dee Brown, *Touch the Earth* edited by T.C. McLuhan, and *The Nevin Shell Heap, Burials and Observations* by Douglas Byers. I recommend them all to you.

Now, how is the Native American spirit helping to change the face of American faith, bringing together East and West, the circle and the cross? Back in 1805 in response to the request of a Christian missionary to preach among the Iroquois, their spokesman, Red Jacket, responded this way:

"Brother, you say that there is but one way to worship and serve the Great Spirit. If there is but one religion, why do you white people differ so much about it? Why not all agree, as you can all read the book?

"Brother, we do not understand these things. We also have a religion which was given to us by our forefathers, and has been handed down to us... We worship in that way. It teaches us to be thankful for all favors we receive; to love each other, and be united. We never quarrel about religion, because it is a matter which concerns each man and the Great Spirit."

During the 1880s and '90s, after the Native way of life had collapsed and most of the Indian wars were over, Wild West shows with "real Indians" became hugely popular entertainment in the U.S., England and Europe. Chiefs visited Washington with regularity and the horseback Plains Indian in eagle feather headdress became a national icon, symbol of a lost golden age. He continued to appear in the popular mind through the early 20th century in movies in which the only good Indians were those who helped the whites do whatever they wanted, or who were conquered and killed.

The year of 1970 was a watershed year in American spirituality falling exactly 100 years after the first Ghost Dance prophet, Tavibo, began preaching out West about the coming green world. Dee Brown of the University of Illinois published *Bury My Heart at Wounded Knee*, a chilling chronicle of the atrocities committed against Native Americans which challenged the history we had been taught in school. Then, Buffy Saint-Marie sang "Now that the Buffalo's Gone" bringing thousands of young Americans to tears of sorrow at the carnage wrought by their forebears. And also in 1970, Lakota author Vine Deloria Jr. published his defiant manifesto, *Custer Died for Your Sins*:

"Our ideas will overcome your ideas. We are going to cut the country's whole value system to shreds. It isn't important that there are only 500,000 of us Indians... What is important is that we have a superior way of life. We Indians have a more human philosophy of life. We Indians will show the country how to act human. What is the ultimate value of a man's life? That is the question."

Today, in spite of a sizable minority of Christians who insist on their own narrow and closed interpretation of the Biblical world-view, there is a vast and growing number of Americans who do not care to 'quarrel about religion' and are open to each others' visions and interpretations, including those of Native Americans. I would go as far as to say that Vine Deloria was right: we are seeing evidence of nothing less than the conversion of the white man.

We are seeing evidence that the great grandchildren of those who fired the cruel Hotchkiss guns at Wounded Knee on the fourth day of Christmas 1890 are now practicing the spirituality of those whom they sought to destroy. What is the evidence? Look around you. The once common saint on the dashboard or cross on the rear-view mirror is replaced by feathers on the dashboard or a circular medicine wheel or dream-catcher on the mirror. In nearly every city and town you will find ecstatic group dancing replacing the staid couples dancing of our parents.

You will find long hair, body ornamentation, handmade jewelry on white men. You will hear the sounds of drumming by white people from coast to coast. You will see pow-wows, smudging, and the revival of ancient indigenous herbal remedies everywhere. You will see a proliferation of totemic animals—wolves, eagles, ravens, dolphins, whales—and increasing respect and compassion for animals wild and domestic.

Rather than the closed-source religion of the Book we are seeing increasingly the open-sourced spirituality of the heart where young and old can dream dreams and share visions, just as among indigenous people since the beginning.

Most powerful of all, we are seeing an explosion of renewed reverence for the earth that started in the souls of aboriginal people and now is shaping the practices of all of us from peasants to Presidents. In short, I believe that we are experiencing a world-wide revival of indigenous spirituality. The ancient world-view that the earth is a living Mother and all creatures are part of one and the same family—all to be loved and cared for—is spreading quietly and peacefully over the whole planet without an arm being lifted in anger. I further believe that, though this world-view may be unlike the teachings of the church, it is very much like the teachings of our own prophets including Jesus himself, but we'll leave that story for another day.

I am not a prophet, but I believe it is safe to say that the melding of indigenous and established religion and the resulting revival will continue, that the prophets and martyrs of the Ghost Dance will one day be honored in the land like those of Christianity, that the earth will continue to turn green, and that we will continue our long journey together.

Postlude

Like you, I suppose, I was raised with the idea that a good formal education was the ticket to a full life. But, I will tell you that despite all my good formal education, had I not gone into small-town ministry, all those classes could have been wasted, and my life would surely have been incalculably poorer than it has been in every way but monetarily. I could very well have reached the end of my little life without ever learning about real life. like the young Buddha, raised in a beautiful walled compound with lovely fruit trees, flowers, and singing birds, so that he would never have to encounter the rougher realities of hunger, disease, old age and death.

If this sort of walled-in life is what you desire for yourself, you probably haven't read this far anyway. However, if you want a fuller and far richer life than you have ever imagined, perhaps what this preacher has said may still be of interest you.

Let us look into the four faces of life that the Buddha discovered and met with compassion when he fled his sheltered and privileged existence. These are hunger, disease, old age, and death, as seen in a small town on the coast of Maine.

First, Hunger. Looking hunger in the face was driving up to the old trailer way out on the Turkey Farm Road surrounded with broken-down cars and appliances and the chained dog in the yard while carrying a couple of bags of groceries; and being welcomed warmly into the cramped, dark interior where several children in third-hand clothes and bare feet gathered curiously around. A spindly, wild Christmas tree cut out in the woods stood over a few presents wrapped in used wrapping paper.

It was gathering boxes of food in the basement of the parsonage back in 1988 and having families drive into our driveway any hour of the day or night in cars that would never again pass inspection for just some food and an encouraging word. It was starting up a food pantry and thrift shop in an old garage, then raising funds and a brand new building on donated land that today serves up to 250 families a week, and this last Thanksgiving served 266 families with food donated by local schools or bought with funds raised by the attached thrift shop.

The grinding poverty is still there, and no better. The problem of poverty in Blue Hill, or the world, will not be solved until we have solved the problem of wealth. We have not done away with hunger yet, but we have not hidden our eyes from it either, and we have learned from it.

Second, Disease. Before becoming a minister I had never visited anyone other than family in a hospital, the last place I ever wanted to be. Now, I know the floor plans, emergency rooms, and intensive care units of all the hospitals within an hour of Blue Hill, including mental hospitals. The ravages of cancer and its treatments, heart disease and its treatments are now familiar experiences, as are the horrors of mental illness, attempted suicide and domestic violence. We have seen treatments that were worse than the disease. We have learned the language of chemotherapy, radiation therapy, electroshock therapy, and psychotherapy. The ravages of physical and mental disease go on unabated. We have not overcome disease, but we have not turned away from it, and it has been our teacher.

Third, Old Age. On the first Sunday of December, we baptized a teary-eyed 88-year-old man—a bird-carver and volunteer for years at the senior citizens meals held twice a week in the church dining room—who had decided that it was "about time" he got baptized. Two days later I visited him in the ICU after his first ever heart attack. (This might understandably make a less idealistic person question baptism for the elderly.) He was soon back in his home and got a new car. There was the newspaper editor and former ambassador to the United Nations who asked the 11-year-old girl also from our church, a superb violinist, to play the Ashokan Farewell for his 96th birthday. Less than a year later, she played it for his funeral.

Old age is the 88-year-old retired school teacher whose garden still produced prolifically and who put up 50-some quarts of vegetables in the fall, and delivered hot meals all over town to elders—some much younger than herself. Old age is the former Navy flier who shoed horses, tended bar, and helped everyone in town until at 72 one rainy night he drove off the road into a boulder and was paralyzed from the shoulders down. We helped raise $30,000 to make his little house suitable. He played chess and bridge all over the world on his computer donated and maintained by the local banjo-playing dentist. We have not overcome old age. We have only been present to it.

Fourth, Death. Historically in any society there have been natural deaths, and un-natural deaths. In a healthy society, natural deaths from disease, old age, or natural disaster far exceed unnatural deaths from murder, starvation, or war. Natural death is not evil, it is a part of life. Yet, today we are expending vast resources to avert natural death among a few of the privileged, while un-natural deaths are increasing exponentially among vast numbers of the under-privileged.

Until I joined the Peninsula Ambulance Corps at age 42, I had never attended a death and never seen a corpse before it had been subjected to the bizarre ministrations of the morticians. That all changed when we were called to carry off a man who had been playing country tunes on his electric keyboard and suddenly fell backwards off his stool, dead. He was the lucky one. We saw his gray, waxen complexion and heard the mourning sounds of his family, so immediate and unmitigated.

"What happened?" I asked.

"He was playing *Make the World Go Away*," said his wife.

Another time, I was called to come over to plan funeral arrangements for a man who was dying at home.

I was met at the door by his wife who said, "His dogs started barking two minutes ago. I think he has died. Would you go in there and see?"

I went to his bedside, pressed my fingers gently to his carotid arteries, and determined that he was gone.

Another time I was called to offer the last rites for a lovely woman with her whole family gathered around the bed where she lay as dead. We said the liturgy and the Lord's Prayer holding hands around her bed.

Then I sat with the bereaved husband at the foot of the bed to discuss final arrangements, at which point the "dead" woman raised her head from the pillow and said, "Hey, you guys, Boo!"

Two nights later we were gathered again for the last rites, and that time they were final. We have not overcome death, but we have been present to it, and taught by it.

The four worldly truths that Siddhartha the Buddha's father tried to hide by keeping his son in a beautiful walled garden correspond strikingly to the Four Horsemen of the Apocalypse described in the fevered visions of the Revelation of John, the last book of the New Testament. Apocalypse (except of the "eco-disaster" genre) is not particularly popular with intellectuals of the PBS/NPR crowd; and is often dismissed off-handedly by them as an obsession of Biblical literalists and NASCAR Christians.

Still, a hard look at the world outside our beautiful garden— the deaths of too many women at the hands of men who claimed to love them, racism in our small towns as we elected our first non-white President, or the perpetual beating of the drums of war in Washington—can send an apocalyptic chill down the spine of the most sanguine intellectual, and make us wonder if that pounding sound in our ears comes, not from hip-hop on some teenager's boom box, or the tympani in Elgar's *Pomp & Circumstance*, but from the galloping hooves of four horrible horsemen bearing down on us.

Here is how the Four Horsemen keep on riding even in the age of the Internet and satellite digital television.

Hunger: Despite the best efforts of international agencies, green revolutions, and genetic engineering, we are told that there are more hungry people in the world today than ever. Moreover, if America's big-rig trucks ever stopped their ceaseless diesel rolling for even a few days, most of us would be mighty hungry as soon as we'd cleaned all the old pasta and pop-tarts out of our cupboards, maybe in three days. It's odd how some will rant about their right to bear arms being taken away by the government when their right to locally-produced food has been taken away by government-supported agri-business with scarcely a whimper from most of the population.

Disease: Who among us over age 55 has not wondered recently if our old smallpox vaccinations are still good? Who among us younger has not wondered where they might get a vaccination? What about dire letters with white powder in them and antibiotic resistant infections? What about HIV-AIDS which is reaching proportions equivalent to the devastating Black Death of the 15th century in some parts of the world?

War: We have been called upon by our government to accept as normal an endless, apocalyptic war against terror. If you look around in our smallest towns you will find memorials to two wars, the Revolutionary War and the Civil War. The first was seen as a war of self-defense against a government that abused and oppressed its people. The second was seen as a war to end the abomination of human slavery. Both of these were, and are still, seen unequivocally as just wars.

True, larger towns will have monuments to the great World Wars of the 20th century. But where are the monuments to the war in Grenada, or the Gulf, or Somalia, or Bosnia, or Iraq? If wars waged not for higher values of justice, but only for our country's strategic and economic advantage become a permanent condition, we will soon lose any remaining reverence for war monuments. Our soldiers, their soldiers, and many more innocents will be dying in the equivalent of massive industrial accidents, or as collateral damage to one nation's mission of world domination.

In the global village of the 21st century it is folly to believe that the few can be saved while the many perish. Yet that is what we have been led to believe.

Like many others, I am convinced that what we are doing in countless small places like Blue Hill has global impact. In literature the term is "synecdoche" in which the part stands metaphorically for the whole. In ecology the phrase is "you can't do just one thing, everything is connected." What we do where we are is what we do in and to the whole world. It's Kant's categorical imperative: Act in such a way that you would want everyone to act in the same way. It's Natural Law. I cannot prove this, I will simply say that this is my profound spiritual conviction.

Maybe you have read *How the Irish Saved Civilization* by Thomas Cahill, describing how the self-sufficient monastic communities in Ireland during the Dark Ages preserved the essentials of a rich culture that was under brutal assault; and how they nursed and carried these seeds through to flower again during the Renaissance and the Enlightenment. It is my conviction that small towns are doing this very thing today.

In small towns in Maine we greet each other, even in passing. You know the "drive-by" wave. One finger off the steering wheel is the basic greeting. Two or three fingers raised show more familiarity. The "whole-hand" wave is reserved for close friends or family, or those we owe money or favors.

On the street, we speak when we pass someone. To not speak means you are from out of town, or that you are simply not on speaking terms. It's common knowledge in small towns and churches that everyone knows everyone else's business. We rejoice when our neighbors rejoice, and we weep when our neighbors weep. When someone accomplishes something, everyone knows about it. It often shows up in the local paper. Did you make the honor roll or get a big promotion or hike the Appalachian Trail from one end to the other? We know, and we congratulate you when we see you. Did you lose a loved one? We know, and we bring casseroles and flowers to your house and we show up at the memorial service.

There is more, of course. Did you get busted for speeding, or worse? It shows up on the police blotter. Did you neglect to pay your taxes? It shows up in the town report. Did you cheat on your wife? Did you act foolish at town meeting? We know, and we gossip about it behind your back, maybe even shun you. In fact, we might shun you for nothing you did, but for something your father or even grandfather did.

Small town and small church life leaves little room for deception or posturing. We know each other so well that there is no point in trying to pretend we're anything but what we are. We are not impressed with credentials or reputations gained elsewhere. We are impressed with hard work and dedication to our town and our values.

There is a healthy conservatism about small town life that honors the way things have been done. The earliest cities appeared in Mesopotamia about 6,000 years ago. Ancient village remains unearthed recently in Israel, date back nearly 20,000 years, and there were doubtless thousands of villages far older that left no evidence. This means we've had far more experience living in villages than in cities, and we've learned the essentials of social survival on this finer scale from long experience. So a certain amount of conservatism is healthy when it preserves this hard-earned ancient wisdom passed down for thousands of years.

The downside of small town conservatism is a stubborn resistance to change or to any truth that bears the slightest hint of originating elsewhere. We've all heard the old story about the newcomer who stood up at town meeting to tell them how it was done in his former hometown. "If it was so good there," was the response, "then why did you leave?"

Jesus, himself, left his hometown and came back with some new ideas. His old neighbors thought his preaching was getting a bit too grandiose, and they said to each other, "Isn't this the son of Joseph the carpenter? Don't we know his family?" Jesus left town muttering, "A prophet is not without honor except in his own country and with his own people."

Change is going to happen regardless, but it can be change for the better or change for the worse. True, too much change can cause people to lose the moorings of their heritage and history. But too little change can cause them to lose their heart and hope and to dwindle and die in the prison of the past.

Villagers avoid these dangers by being mostly generalists, not specialists. They may have their own favored trade, but they know many. Around here this means seasonal work like fishing, blueberry raking, hunting, tipping, wreath-making, working in the woods and then fishing again. It means knowing a lot about a lot of things and a little about everything. When Raymond Robertson, aged 85, said to me once, "I used to know one hell of a lot but I've forgotten most of it," he was only half joking.

This sort of generalized knowledge also means that the information needed for survival is not the property of a few. It is distributed through the community and available to anyone willing to ask. Small town knowledge is also open-sourced, that is, it is constantly being reviewed and corrected and can be added to by anyone who is respected for what they do. The source of knowledge is mostly experience rather than study. That gives small town knowledge an advantage: which is, it works. New knowledge, once it passes this test, is readily adopted.

A few elders in town may know just about everything about the town, and if they don't know, they know someone who does.

What we call 'gossip' or 'the grapevine' is a living body of knowledge that grows and changes, at the post office, the job-site, the hardware store, the town hall, the hair-dresser, the market, and wherever people gather. Fishing, building, farming, gardening, animal care, treatment of sickness and injury, cooking, preserving, pruning, who is trustworthy and who is not; volumes of knowledge are available to the respectfully inquisitive villager. At its best, this small town knowledge is like a living thing: practical, resilient, self-correcting, growing, evolving. Unlike a living thing, it may live nearly forever.

I remember talking for hours with Effie Hinckley who at 100 was blind and nearly deaf, but still bright as a new penny. She knitted mittens by feel, counting the stitches with her fingers. Her grand-daughter told me that all Effie's great-grandchildren still have a life-time supply of mittens tucked into their closets.

When I came to visit, the first thing Effie wanted was for me to sit next to her and shout into her ear the news from town. She told me stories her grandmother had told her about Jonathan Fisher who came to town in 1796 and died in 1847. When Father Fisher came to visit the schoolhouse, the teacher would tell the children to put on their shoes and be prepared to recite their lessons faultlessly for the minister. Effie told these stories with delight from her nearly 200-year-old oral encyclopedia of local knowledge, history and wisdom for living.

Though the reader will certainly have concluded by now that I have a raging, if not blinding, bias in favor of small towns, I am not going to declare here that small town life will one day save civilization, because that might prove to be hog-wash. But, I will say that our small towns, small churches, and small schools are caretakers of a rich heirloom seed-bank of viable human values which have been tried and tested in towns and villages around the world for thousands of years, long before the first city appeared. We are keeping alive some very old, very vigorous strains of community life that will one day be available to inoculate and heal the diseases of venality, violence, materialism and meaninglessness which have infected the world body and are making it mortally ill.

These healthy seeds of community life are beginning to find their way into post-modern awareness with a deliciously ironic twist. The ancient tribal council which evolved into the church and town meeting, lo and behold, is now touted as an innovative form of "participatory democracy." The ageless value of thrift with its motto, "Waste not, want not," is updated into the 21st century as "economy of scale." The old aphorism of our great-grandparents: "Use it up, wear it out, make it do, or do without," is now put forth as a trendy "voluntary simplicity." The tribal hunting ground or pasture which evolved into the village commons is now presented as a "green zone" or a "land trust." Ancestral places of worship are now "voluntary spiritual communities" and "faith-based organizations." Old-fashioned natural home remedies are resurrected as "alternative medicine."

The Ancient and Honorable Fire Company is now raised up under the self-conscious rubric of "volunteerism." The perennial potluck public supper to which everyone brings what they can and eats all they want, with the left-overs sent home with someone who needs them, is now hailed as "cooperative local economy." The old practice of getting your eggs, milk, meat and vegetables from your garden and your neighbors is now touted as "community-based agriculture." And yet, small towns and villages have been doing these things for more than 20 millennia. It's very old, very good, and very simple, really.

Computers and cell phones are fascinating, the Internet is fine, parking garages and skyscrapers and space shuttles are amazing, but in the end you can't feed them to your children.

Power, celebrity, wealth and fame have always mocked and ridiculed the small-town ways of service, simplicity, self-sufficiency and serenity; to the point that self-obsession and self-aggrandizement gravely threaten the human experiment.

Thomas Gray (1716-1771) wrote in his "Elegy in a Country Church-yard":

Let not Ambition mock their useful toil,
Their homely joys and destiny obscure;
Nor Grandeur hear with a disdainful smile
The short and simple annals of the poor.
The boast of heraldry, the pomp of power,
And all that beauty, all that wealth e'er gave,
Awaits alike the inevitable hour.
The paths of glory lead but to the grave.

Another small town boy, Henry David Thoreau of Concord, Massachusetts, wrote in his journal on January 24, 1856:

"I have seen a collection of stately elms which better
deserved to be represented at the general court than the
manikins beneath. They look from township to township.
They battle with the tempests of a century. See what scars
they bear, what limbs they lost before we were born. Yet
they never adjourn, they steadily vote for their principles
and send their roots further and further from the same
center... They combine a true radicalism with a true
conservatism. Their conservatism is... a solid heartwood...
forever by its support assisting to extend the area of their
radicalism"

This could be dismissed easily as nostalgia for a forgotten past, except for one undeniable fact: There are presently literally thousands of small towns and villages world-wide still holding to and thriving with their ancient conservative radical values, still striving to provide a good life for their children and elders, still leaving their houses unlocked, still in touch with their neighbors, carrying on through the ages, through war and peace, through the rise and fall of great cities and empires, through drought, famine, fire, flood, panic, boom and bust.

Poet Gary Snyder is fond of saying, "Sometimes the most radical thing you can do is stay in one place." After the family, the village is the oldest human institution on earth. And today there are thousands of disenchanted urbanites and suburbanites flocking to these shrines of ancient wisdom for the well-being of themselves and their children. Many have found, and still find, a calling to labor daily in local agriculture, churches, schools and town government in these small nurseries of human well-being, our truest insurance into the future.

When all is said and done, there can be no more fair and fitting thing than this to do with your education, your gifts, your one mortal life, and your one immortal soul.

About the Author

Rob McCall, a graduate of Harvard Divinity School, has long served as the minister of the First Congregational Church in Blue Hill, Maine. His weekly radio commentaries are heard throughout Maine and at www.weru.org.